WRITERS AND THEIR WORK

ISOBEL ARMSTRONG
*General Editor*

# ANGELA CARTER

# ANGELA CARTER

## Lorna Sage

### Second edition

101756
823CAR

© Copyright 1994 and 2007 by Lorna Sage
Revised bibliography © 2007 by Dr. Eleni Seliniadou

First published in 1994 by Northcote House Publishers Ltd, Horndon, Tavistock,
Devon, PL19 9NQ, United Kingdom.
Tel: +44 (0) 1822 810066  Fax: +44 (0) 1822 810034.

Second edition 2007

**British Library Cataloguing-in-Publication Data**
A catalogue record for this book is available from the British Library

ISBN 0 7463 1145 1

Typeset by PDQ Typesetting, Newcastle-under-Lyme
Printed and bound in the United Kingdom by Athenaeum Press Ltd, Gateshead,
Tyne & Wear

For my grand-daughter Olivia

# Contents

# Acknowledgements

An early version of some of the biographical material first appeared in *Granta*, 41 1992, an issue devoted to biography.

The author and the publishers are also pleased to acknowledge the inclusion of quotations from Angela Carter's own work as well as from interviews and a number of media sources all of which are cited in detail in the bibliography. Quotations from her personal letters are published with grateful acknowledgement to the estate of Angela Carter, administered by Rogers, Coleridge & White, 20 Powis Mews, London W11 1JN.

# Biographical Outline

| | |
|---|---|
| 1940 | Born Angela Olive Stalker, 7 May, Eastbourne, Sussex; spends the war in Yorkshire with her maternal grandmother; educated direct grant school in Balham. |
| 1959 | Junior reporter, *Croydon Advertiser*. |
| 1960 | Marries Paul Carter. |
| 1962–5 | Reads English at the University of Bristol, specializing in the medieval period. |
| 1966 | First novel, *Shadow Dance*, published. |
| 1967 | Wins John Llewellyn Rhys prize for second novel, *The Magic Toyshop*. |
| 1968 | Wins Somerset Maugham Award for third novel, *Several Perceptions*. |
| 1969–72 | Visits, then lives in, Japan, working briefly for NHK Broadcasting Company; sending articles back to *New Society*. |
| 1972 | Divorced from Paul Carter. |
| 1976–8 | Arts Council for Great Britain Fellow in Sheffield. |
| 1977– | Settles in South London, with Mark Pearce; member of Virago advisory board; Virago commission *The Sadeian Woman* (1979). |
| 1980–1 | Visiting Professor on the Writing Programme at Brown University, Providence, Rhode Island, USA, substituting for John Hawkes. |
| 1983 | Son Alexander Pearce born. |
| 1984 | Writer in residence, University of Adelaide, South Australia: *Company of Wolves* (based on *The Bloody Chamber* (1979)) released on film; *Nights at the Circus* published by Chatto & Windus (joint winner of the James Tait Black Memorial Prize for 1985). |

1984–7 Teaches part-time on the Writing MA at the University of East Anglia in Norwich.

1991 Publishes her last novel, *Wise Children*.

1992 Dies, 16 February.

# Abbreviations and References

| | |
|---|---|
| BC | *The Bloody Chamber and Other Stories* (London: Gollancz, 1979) |
| BV | *Black Venus* (London: Chatto & Windus, 1985) |
| CP | *The Fairy Tales of Charles Perrault* (New York: Bard Books, 1979) |
| DRH | *The Infernal Desire Machines of Doctor Hoffman* (1972: repr. as *The War of Dreams*, New York: Bard Books, 1977) |
| F. | 'Sugar Daddy' in Ursula Owen (ed.), *Fathers* (London: Virago, 1983), 20–30 |
| FL | 'Family Life' – 6, Time to Tell the Time, *New Review*, 4/42 (Sept. 1977), 41–6 |
| FT | *The Virago Book of Fairy Tales* (London: Virago, 1990) |
| FW | *Fireworks* (London: Virago, 1988) |
| HV | *Heroes and Villains* (Harmondsworth: Penguin, 1981) |
| L. | *Love* (London: Rupert Hart-Davis, 1971) |
| LO | *Love* (revised edn., London: Chatto & Windus, 1987) |
| MT | *The Magic Toyshop* (London: Virago, 1981) |
| NC | *Nights at the Circus* (London: Chatto & Windus, 1984) |
| NFL | 'Notes from the Front Line', in Michelene Wandor (ed.), *On Gender and Writing* (London: Pandora Press, 1983), 69–77 |
| NS | *Nothing Sacred: Selected Writings* (London: Virago 1982) |
| NW | Lorna Sage, 'Angela Carter Interviewed by Lorna Sage', in Malcolm Bradbury and Judith Cooke (eds.), *New Writing* (London: Minerva Press, 1992) 185–93 |
| PNE | *The Passion of New Eve* (London: Virago, 1982) |
| QM | 'The Quilt Maker', in *Sex and Sensibility: Stories by Contemporary Women Writers from Nine Countries* (London: Sidgwick & Jackson, 1981), 119–40 |

| | |
|---|---|
| SD | *Shadow Dance* (1966) repr. as *Honeybuzzard*, (London: Pan Books, 1968) |
| SP | *Several Perceptions* (London: Heinemann, 1968) |
| SS | Lorna Sage, 'The Savage Sideshow', *New Review* (4/39–40 (1977), 51–7 |
| SW | *The Sadeian Woman: An Exercise in Cultural History* (London: Virago, 1979) |
| WC | *Wise Children* (London: Chatto & Windus, 1991) |
| YO | 'Truly, It Felt Like Year One', in Sara Maitland (ed.), *Very Heaven: Looking Back at the 1960s* (London: Virago, 1988) 209–16 |
| YS | *Come Unto These Yellow Sands: Four Radio Plays* (Newcastle upon Tyne: Bloodaxe Books, 1985) |

# Prologue

When Angela Carter died in 1992, at the age of 51, the obituaries nearly all agreed on one thing – that she was a spell-binder. This is Canadian novelist Margaret Atwood:

> The amazing thing about her, for me, was that someone who looked so much like the Fairy Godmother – the long, prematurely-white hair, the beautiful complexion, the benign, slightly blinky eyes, the heart-shaped mouth – should actually *be* so much like the Fairy Godmother. She seemed always on the verge of bestowing something – some talisman, some magic token you'd need to get through the dark forest, some verbal formula useful for the opening of charmed doors.

Her friend and publisher Carmen Callil (Virago, Chatto) paid her the same kind of tribute: 'She had flotillas of friends. . . . Once you were in you were part of an enchanted circle. . . . She was the oracle we all consulted, a listener whose eloquent silences kept us hanging on every word she quietly and wickedly uttered.' This picture of her as a witch or wise woman derives not only from her personality in private life, but from the role she evolved for herself as a writer, on the page, and even more as a performer of her own work in readings, when she could reconnect herself with the oral tradition of story-telling.

In fact you cannot, in the end, separate the woman and the writer. One of Angela Carter's most impressive and humorous achievements was that she evolved this part to play. How to Be the Woman Writer. Not that she was wearing a mask, exactly; it was more a matter of refusing to observe any decorous distinction between art and life, so that she was inventive in reality as well as in creating plots and characters for the books. She belongs among the fabulists and tale-spinners, the mockers and speculators and iconoclasts and utopians. 'She was born subversive,' Margaret Atwood wrote: 'She had an instinctive feeling for the other side, which included also the underside.'[1]

She was born in 1940, and grew up in south London in the post-war period of free orange juice and cod-liver oil, the National Health Service, and grammar-school education, when children's sweets were rationed and their mothers were encouraged to go back home and be housewives. In the 1950s, when she was in her teens, the prevailing style of British writing and of film-making (and of grey-and-white television) was neo-realistic – of a piece with the general atmosphere of austerity. Rebellion itself (the Beats in America, existentialists in France, 'Angry Young Men' in Britain) took the form of a quest for authenticity and (mostly male) mobility and freedom. And the other side of *that* was a growing sense that realism and authenticity were somehow subtly fake, threadbare, conformist even when they seemed not to be. The anti-novel, the *nouveau roman*, fantastic tales, and satires on sincerity all gained ground, though there was no real consensus about how to label them or think about them, no movement you could join.

In any case, not much of this was happening in England; experiment was un-English, somehow. Angela Carter in the long run proved very interested in the question of what it meant to be English, but earlier on she found herself looking to outsiders of all sorts for inspiration. She would have said that this was entirely appropriate: she was a great believer in the kind of reverse-anthropology which involves studying your own culture as if from elsewhere, cultivating the viewpoint of an alien in order to defamiliarize the landscape of habit. She was very much attracted to the work of Symbolist and Dadaist artists, and liked to underline her estrangement from the glum poetry of domestic complaint: 'Anybody who had a stiff injection of Rimbaud at 18 isn't going to be able to cope very well with Philip Larkin, I'm afraid. There must be more to life than this one says. It made the circumstances of my everyday life profoundly unsatisfactory. Later the surrealists had the same effect' (SS 54). French structuralist thinkers (Claude Lévi-Strauss, Roland Barthes, Michel Foucault) were important to her too, because they provided an armour of theory she could call on to protect her creative intuitions. She was fascinated, in particular, by the idea that writing was an act that took you out of your own skin, out of your background, gender, class, nationality...

There is thus a certain paradox in talking about her work in the context of her life, and her character. But I do not propose to be deterred from doing just that, since I want to argue that the 1968 proclamation of 'The Death of the Author' (Barthes's phrase) was very much part of a generation's collective life story. This is how Barthes expressed their desire to find anonymity in the written word: 'writing is the destruction of every voice, of every point of origin. Writing is that neutral, composite, oblique space where our subject slips away, the negative where all identity is lost, starting with the very identity of the body writing.'[2] Losing yourself was one of Liberation's first moves, and it had a special charm for gay men like Barthes and for bloody-minded women like Carter. If you renounced and denied the author's power over the text, the author's traditional authority, you were symbolically defying too the patriarchal power that decreed *your* place in the book of the world. 'We know now', wrote Barthes in 'The Death of the Author', 'that a text is not a line of words releasing a single "theological" meaning (the "message" of the Author-God) but a multi-dimensional space.'[3] The Author-God, and authors who took after Him, were seen as (among other things) enemies of sexual revolution, agents of the gender-police, Father-figures behind the conspiracy to present us with a solid, Natural world-picture.

Carter, looking back, recaptured some of the euphoria of spitting in Almighty conformity's eye:

> truly, it felt like Year One ... all that was holy was in the process of being profaned.... I can date to that time ... and to that sense of heightened awareness of the society around me in the summer of 1968, my own questioning of the nature of my reality as a *woman*. How that social fiction of my 'femininity' was created, by means outside my control, and palmed off on me as the real thing. (NFL 70)

She went on, however – she was writing in 1983 – to qualify the 'sense of limitless freedom' you get by sloughing off the myths, with a sentence which reinstates with a vengeance the determinations of history: 'I am the pure product of an advanced, industrialised, post-imperialist country in decline' (NFL 73). This is deliberately, provocatively overstated, but she meant it none the less. In fact, it is a remark that captures her tone pretty exactly: I can just see the *moue* of amused disgust (but also *disgusted* disgust at the same time, morally and intellectually fastidious disgust) with which she would greet the notion that you could somehow levitate out of history.

Taking into account the writer's life doesn't mean that you have to reinvent your subject as a 'real' person. Angela Carter's life – the background of social mobility, the teenage anorexia, the education and self-education into the deliquescent riches of the ruins of various great traditions, the early marriage and divorce, the role-playing and shape-shifting, the travels, the choice of a man much younger, the baby in her forties – is the story of someone walking a tightrope. It is all happening 'on the edge', in no-man's land, among the debris left by past convictions. By the end, her life fitted her more or less like a glove, but that was because she had put it together, by trial and error, *bricolage*, all in the (conventionally) wrong order. Her genius for estrangement came out of a thin-skinned extremity of response to the circumstances of her life, and to the signs of the times. She was, indeed, literally thin-skinned: her skin was very fair, pink and white, she weathered quite a bit but never tanned, and you could see the veins easily. You might almost say her body thought. She had very good bones, and was photogenic, so that it didn't matter that she'd stopped looking in mirrors and painting her face. She let her hair grow out white in wisps two or three years before she got pregnant. I knew her well from the mid-1970s on, and inevitably that colours my picture of her, and my sense that she lived by her own rules, and took her own time, more than most of us manage. I could have been a grandmother by the time she was a mother, and I was younger than she. The shape a woman's life takes now is a lot less determined than once it was. Or: the determinations are more subtle, you are *sentenced* to assemble your own version.

# 1

# Beginning

There's a theory, one I find persuasive, that the quest for knowledge is, at bottom, the search for the answer to the question 'Where was I before I was born?'
    In the beginning was . . . what?
    Perhaps, in the beginning, there was a curious room, a room like this one, crammed with wonders.

Angela Carter, 'The Curious Room' (1990)[1]

Angela Carter cultivated the role of fairy godmother and/or witch, and – in *The Bloody Chamber* (1979) – rewrote the Bluebeard story with pistol-toting Mother riding to the rescue at the last minute. However, it was not her own mother, one of a family of 'great examination-passers' (a scholarship girl who had left school at 15, to work at Selfridges in what was then acceptably genteel fashion, as a sales lady), who provided the model for this kind of figure, but her maternal grandmother, who had come originally from south Yorkshire. Granny came to the rescue in the year of Angela's birth (1940), and evacuated herself and her grand-children from south London back to the gritty coal-mining village of Wath-upon-Dearne, kidnapping them safely into the past for the duration of the war.

Skipping a generation took Angela back to 'Votes for Women', working class radicalism, outside lavatories, and coal-dust coughs. Granny ought, perhaps, to have surfaced in the fiction as the spirit of social realism – though actually it makes sense that she is in the magical mode, since her brand of eccentric toughness was already thoroughly archaic from the point of view of the post-war and the south. In Angela's last novel, *Wise Children*, the granny-figure is killed in the blitz, but bequeaths to her adoptive granddaughters Dora and Nora (possibly her natural daughters?) the Brixton house that offers them a safe haven when they have to

5

retire from the stage. 'When the bombardments began, Grandma would go outside and shake her fist at the old men in the sky.... She was our air-raid shelter; she was our entertainment; she was our breast', says Dora (WC 29).

Expanding on this theme in a late interview, Carter said that she had often been asked why there were so few mothers in her books, and had realized that in her imaginative topography houses stood in for mothers: 'When mother is dead, all the life has gone out of the house. The shop in *The Magic Toyshop* gets burnt down, the old dark house, and adult life begins. In this novel [*Wise Children*], though either way mother is dead, her spirit lives on and the house survives. I don't think it's anything to do with *my* mother, but the kind of power mothers have is enormous' (*NW* 190). This symbolic weight attaches itself to Grandma, for her. It is Grandma who presides over the matriarchal space of the Carter house of fiction. In a *New Review* series on 'Family Life' back in 1976, Angela wrote that her grandmother

> was a woman of such physical and spiritual heaviness she seemed to have been born with a greater degree of gravity than most people. She came from a community where women rule the roost.... Her personality had an architectonic quality; I think of her when I see some of the great London railway termini, especially Saint Pancras, with its soot and turrets, and she overshadowed her own daughters, whom she did not understand – my mother, who liked things to be nice; my dotty aunt. (FL 43–4)

If Grandmother is a larger-than-life 'character' for her – Leninist Lizzie the heroine's minder in *Nights at the Circus* looks like another avatar – then mother is almost a missing person.

This was not at all unusual, particularly for daughters growing up in the 1940s and 1950s, with upwardly socially mobile mothers who had given up work, women girlified, exiled, and isolated in domesticity, who had not 'done anything' with their education. She wrote about her Scottish journalist father with obvious pleasure – 'very little ... to do with the stern fearful face of the Father in patriarchy.... there was no fear' (F. 26–7). But about her mother, who was younger but died first, she was wry, oblique, regretful, protective: 'There was to be no struggle for my mother, who married herself young to an adoring husband who indulged her, who was subject to ill-health, who spoke standard English, who continued to wear fancy clothes' (FL 44). Angela was supposed to do something with her own education, so instead, of course, she married young herself, in reaction against what her mother wanted for her, though it didn't last long. And if you look for the provenance of the feminist writer, mother is the key too. Rosalind Coward generalizes the point in *Our Treacherous Hearts*:

> Feminism is almost invariably seen as a struggle – or head-on collision – with men. But the truth is that the deep struggle of feminism was with the previous generation of women. Feminism could be called the daughters' revolt, so central has been the issue of women defining themselves against the previous generation and distancing themselves from their mothers. [2]

The women who really nailed patriarchy were not on the whole the ones with authoritarian fathers, but the ones with troubled, contradictory mothers: you aim your feminism less against men, than against the picture of the woman you don't want to be, the enemy within. In this case, the girl-wife. Mother was exigent as well as fragile, however. She read a lot, and took bookishness for granted: 'when I'd had some novels published, and my mother had been prowling around I think Harrods book department, and she'd noticed that my books were on the same display as Iris Murdoch's, she said to me, "I suppose you think that makes you an intellectual?"' (SS 54). Mother kept up *her* family's Labour convictions, too. When Angela's father died, in 1988, at 92, after nearly twenty years as a widower, she wrote in a letter: 'The only bright spot is, I found the old bugger's membership card – Scottish Conservative Party! God, my mum will give him a good talking-to on the other side. Nevertheless, his demise means that the Scottish Conservative Party's membership has now dropped by 50%. Cold comfort, cold comfort.' She liked the idea that she had extended the span of generations, grandfather to grandson, by having her son Alexander so late. And her ambivalent feelings towards her mother had already supplied her with a motive for skipping a female generation, in imagination. Back to Gran.

It wasn't a card she played openly until she got older, when she took to fairy tales and ribaldry. However, the whole *self-conscious* quality of her 1960s début derives from this sense of a (lost, deliberately distanced) reality: working class, northern, matriarchal. None of this could she *be*, or speak directly for, but she could do it in pastiche – and she did, writing in ghostly quotation marks. If there was nearly nothing 'natural' about her style, this was because her kind of family background introduced you early on to the notion that the culture was a dressing-up box, and to the bliss and nightmare of turning the clock back. Even her maternal grandfather, who had died before she was born, and who had been in the Indian Army in his youth, contributed to the inventory of Grandma's trophies: 'gran's house was full of relics of Empire, ebony elephants, spears, a carved coconut shell representing the Hindu cosmogony, beautiful shells from tropic seas' (FL 43).

Revisiting the past, and a different social order, is what her second novel, *The Magic Toyshop* (1967), is about – slipping out of your precarious middle-classness into the house of (superficial) horrors but (libidinal) mirrors. Ten years after its publication she said to me in interview – I had asked, 'Do you think your environment shaped you?':

> Well, my brother and I speculate endlessly on this point. We often say to one another, How is it possible such camp little flowers as ourselves emanated from Balham via Wath-upon-Dearne and the places my father comes from, north Aberdeenshire, stark, bleak and apparently lugubriously Calvinistic, witch-burning country? But obviously, something in this peculiar rootless, upward, downward, sideways socially mobile family, living in twilight zones. (SS 53).

The operative phrase here is 'camp little flowers'. In one sense, it simply signals 'artiness': her elder brother Hugh became a musician (he taught music for many years), and she herself, after a brief apprenticeship in journalism, went to university (Bristol) and became, of course, a writer. But there is more to it than that. In *The Magic Toyshop* sinister Uncle Philip is surnamed 'Flower', as if she was making a private joke along these lines; and in her third book, *Several Perceptions* (1968), the limping anti-heroine, an obdurate orphan, has been given the thoroughly inappropriate surname 'Blossom'. 'Camp' repays further attention, too: it was one of the 1960s names for the taste for excess and mockery that characterized her early books, and a notoriously slippery term.

Susan Sontag's 1964 essay 'Notes on Camp' described the relevant sensibility, without giving up on the slipperiness:

> even though homosexuals have been its vanguard, Camp taste is much more than homosexual taste. Obviously, its metaphor of life as theatre is peculiarly suited as a justification and projection of a certain

aspect of the situation of homosexuals.... Yet one feels that if homosexuals hadn't more or less invented Camp, someone else would.[3]

Women artists and critics who felt imprisoned in the roles assigned them in 'reality', for instance? Sontag, like Carter, was fascinated by Camp because it represented a kind of fault-line running through contemporary culture, where the binary opposition of masculine and feminine broke down. Camp mocked at seriousness, sincerity, authenticity (in any case values established and guaranteed largely by the male avant-garde). What existentialists labelled 'bad faith' and deplored, camp taste enjoyed and admired as (Sontag's phrase) 'the theatricalization of experience': 'Camp sees everything in quotation marks. It's not a lamp, but a "lamp"; not a woman, but a "woman". To perceive Camp in objects and persons is to understand Being-as-Playing-a-Role. It is the farthest extension, in sensibility, of the metaphor of life as theatre.'[4] Compare Carter (above) on her 1960s questioning 'of the nature of my reality as a *woman*. How that social fiction of my "femininity" was created.' In Carter's early fiction, people dress up (or down) to *play themselves*; they parade their characters as 'acts'. This is what Sontag calls 'Dandyism in the age of mass culture', and England briefly cornered the market in it in the 1960s – partly because in this country we were perforce living in the past, or at least among the ruins of past greatness. And as Sontag (again) puts it, 'so many of the objects prized by Camp taste are old-fashioned, out-of-date, *demodé*. It's not a love of the old as such. It's simply that the process of aging or deterioration provides the necessary detachment.'[5] In very much the same spirit, Carter's fiction starts off among the past's debris. This is not a matter of nostalgia, but connects with a quite different contemporary sensation: of coming at the end, mopping up, having the freedom of *anomie*.

Angela Carter completed her first novel *Shadow Dance* (later renamed *Honeybuzzard*, after its sexy and malign master of ceremonies, in American and paperback versions) during her second summer vacation as a student of literature at Bristol, in 1964. As first books often do, it crammed in ideas and themes and images that its author was to explore at leisure for years to come. For that very reason, and because it marks the cultural moment where she 'came in', *Shadow Dance* deserves some space. It was a shocking book when it was published in 1966, and still is – perhaps more so in some ways than it was at the time, since its treatment of sexual politics is quite ruthlessly of its era. Just as in the separate-spheres domain of Jane Austen's novels you never have any extended scene which shows men alone together, so in this sexually liberated book there is never any scene between women alone: the female characters are scattered at large in a man's world. At the novel's centre are two young men, dark brooding Morris – from whose point of view the story is told – and beautiful, blond Honeybuzzard. They are in business together, running a junk shop and scavenging in deserted houses for goodies, and they also have in common Ghislaine – a baby-doll girl, white and cold and sweet like ice-cream, who once upon a time cut a swathe through the whole male world of the book until Morris, after a disastrous one-night stand with her, asked Honey to 'teach her a lesson' and he did. Though no one knows for sure, everyone takes for granted that it was Honeybuzzard who sliced up Ghislaine's beautiful face.

It is when the new monstrously-scarred Ghislaine reappears and accosts an appalled Morris in the pub, with all her stitch-marks showing ('the bride of Frankenstein'), that the book opens. The very first words set the Camp tone, unmistakably: 'The bar was a mock-up, a forgery, a fake: an ad-man's crazy dream of a Spanish patio.' On to this set steps Ghislaine, revisiting like a ghoul the scene of her former triumphs:

> She used to come here, every night.... and she gathered them up in armfuls, her lovers, every night, in the manner of a careless baby playing in a meadow, pulling both flowers and grass and nettles and piss-the-beds in a spilling, promiscuous bundle. 'She is a burning child, a fiery bud,' said Honeybuzzard, before he knifed her. All the clichés fitted her; candleflame for moths, a fire that burned those around her but was not itself consumed. And now her face was all sideways and might suddenly ... leak gallons of blood and drown them all, and herself, too. (*SD* 7)

She is imagined as one of the undead, the victim as predator. She is Dracula's bride when she's not playing Frankenstein's (the atmosphere belongs to Hammer horror films, anyway pretty interchangeable), and the pain of her condition is matched only by its stylization. She acts her anguish as she suffers; it is no wonder that Morris's guilty dreams take place in a mental *theatre*.

10

'He dreamed he was cutting her face with a jagged shard of broken glass.... There was a gallery of people watching them and applauding sporadically, like the audience at a cricket match' (*SD* 20–1). Ghislaine will become the perfect – perfectly perverse – go-between for Morris and Honey, as she enters on her masochistic quest for yet more suffering.

She comes to stand for the Past itself, a vengeful emissary from the realm of shadows Morris and Honey regularly raid. Even in her pristine state she was second-hand, imitation, an android, a 'ravishing automaton' (*SD* 7) with her 'personalised, patented laugh' (*SD* 10). Now that she is so grotesquely mutilated she suggests to Morris 'a Francis Bacon painting of flesh as a disgusting symbol of the human condition' (*SD* 22). He avoids her like the plague, but she invades his dreams: 'invisible old woman of the sea, all ugly and piteous, she went with him, clutching him with her white legs and her long slender arms' (*SD* 37). In short, she is entirely saturated with ready-made meanings, and that is what makes her truly the book's nightmare-heroine and incubus.

For this is a whole world of leftovers, quotes, copies, *déjà vu*: 'life imitating rotten art again, as Honey always said it did' (*SD* 10). Morris, who is supposed to be a painter, but despises his own work and has settled for collecting junk instead (the borders between art and trash, life and death, are busily dissolving), admires Honeybuzzard for his pitiless playfulness. Honey is as beautiful as Ghislaine was, but he is a sadistic joker and power addict (' "They are all shadows" ' (*SD* 55)), the one who pulls other people's strings (' "I should like ... to play chess with men and women" ' (*SD* 112)). He becomes a toy-maker, making jumping-jack caricatures of the other characters (anticipating sinister Uncle Philip Flower in *The Magic Toyshop*), and fantasizing about the freedom of role-playing:

'I like – you know – to slip in and out of me. I would like to be somebody different each morning. Me and not-me. I would like to have a cupboard bulging with all different bodies and faces.... There was a man, last night; we were in a club and there was this man, singing blues, and he had a red rose stuck in his shirt. It was red as the cap of liberty.... I would like to wear him, tomorrow morning.' (*SD* 76).

Honey plays tirelessly and cruelly, like a big cat; anything and anyone is fair game. He shares the vampire imagery with Ghislaine

– but the reference (above) to the 'cap of liberty' worn in the French Revolution signals that he is no ordinary monster. Like the Marquis de Sade, he is a radical pornographer, who strips away the mystifications of sex and sentiment to reveal the workings of power underneath. He camps it up, too: ' "Never been so embarrassed, darling." He made a mincing gesture with his right hand and tittered' (*SD* 60) – and is regularly described in androgynous terms. He bows to no conventions about masculine Nature.

It is Camp with a capital 'C' that matters here, though, and to understand Honeybuzzard's dubious charm for his creator, as well as for characters in the book, you have to recognize that he alone belongs to two worlds, in gender terms and, in terms just as vital to Carter the writer, the real (life) and the shadow (art). He is on that fault-line, an early embodiment of her conviction that the fantastical and the actual can exist in the same plane. The Gothic need not be locked away in a separate *genre*. Honey is in the real world, very much the kind of figure Sontag described, 'a dandy in the age of mass culture': 'Camp taste transcends the nausea of the replica.... The relation between boredom and Camp taste cannot be overestimated. Camp taste is by its nature possible only in affluent societies, in societies or circles capable of experiencing the psychopathology of affluence.'[6] When Honey and Morris strip old houses, sell beaded frocks and chipped Staffordshire china and kitsch loo-chains, they are located securely in their Sixties moment, they are 'realistic' figures. But they also, like Ghislaine, point to the pull of the past, the spectre that faced Carter from the very beginning of her writing career – the thought that there was nothing new to do, or be: 'I am the pure product of an advanced, industrialised, post-imperialist country in decline.' *Shadow Dance* dramatizes the paradoxical advantages of living in a belated world – you can see people as constructs, not born but made; you have to piece together your own myths, in the absence of God-given truths.

In the plot the Past devours the three main characters. Morris cannot resist 'the smell of dirt, poverty and graveclothes.... He loved the smell. He loved junk' (*SD* 25). He and Honeybuzzard achieve a most dangerous moment of closeness waltzing together – a joke that turns serious – in a mirrored room in a condemned house: 'Their reflections merged together, rippling on the dark surface of the mirror ... spinning between the waltzing walls....

But when the time came for parting and bowing and curtseying to one another, Honeybuzzard instead crushed his partner in a fierce embrace ... wet mouth fastened on his throat' (SD 90). Later, in another, strangely churchy derelict mansion, with 'a snaggle of rosaries in a corner' and a tortured Christ 'fallen from the wall', Honeybuzzard muses viciously about the two of them taking turns to lay Ghislaine on the crucifix: ' "you know her father's a clergyman? ... she wrote to me that it was a spiritual defloration when I knifed her" ' (SD 124–6). This more or less completes the symbolic 'nailing' of Ghislaine. She represents all little girls made of sugar-and-spice and all things nice, and her father is an agent of the Almighty, hence she becomes Honey's sacrificial lamb. In mutilating and destroying her he is profaning all that is (supposed to be) holy. She wins too, in a way, since she offers him an invitation he cannot refuse – ' "you are my master, do what you like with me" ' – and, power-drunk, he descends into madness and murders her, laying her body out in the ruined church-house. Morris, reeling with the horror of it, none the less is fatally fascinated:

> To go back into the house, forsaking the clear light ... and the sweet clean breeze; to enter, Orpheus-like, the shadowed regions of death.... in this new dimension outside both time and space he, Morris, could truly be heroic....
> Morris vanished into the shadows. (SD 171–2)

These are the last words of *Shadow Dance*.

There is little doubt that Carter shares her characters' obsession with the realm of shades, of past realities ruined and recycled and reproduced and represented. The dressing-up box is where she begins; she *begins* with ends. She finds inspiration precisely in the (un)deadness of Gothic and grotesque properties. 'I do think', she would say later, 'we're at the end of a line, and to a certain extent I'm making a conscious critique of the culture I was born to. In a period like this of transition and conflicting ideologies, when there isn't a prevalent ideology, really all artists can do is go round mopping up' (SS 56). There was vital food for imagination in the shadows.

And, in any case, this first novel is full of unfinished business – figures and ideas that spell hope in the midst of the underworld gloom. Honeybuzzard's London girlfriend Emily, for instance, is more than the dolly-bird she at first seems: she recovers from his betrayal with great speed, and takes in her stride, too, the discovery that she is pregnant. She is a new-style matriarch (or patriarch even, thinks Morris – she has her own androgynous aspect), tough as old boots, a survivor. Morris, who judges her mentally blank, is taken by surprise by a sudden glimpse of the way her brain is furnished:

'I found this key in one of his trouser pockets, see, and I thought, you know, of Bluebeard.'
'Bluebeard?'
'Bluebeard. And the locked room. I don't know him very well, you know. And Sister Anne, Sister Anne, what do you see...' (SD 100).

Emily is marginal to this book, but she will come into her own in Carter's future writing – in the cool heroines of *The Magic Toyshop* and *Heroes and Villains*, and the bride who outwits Bluebeard in *The Bloody Chamber* (1979).

Another loose end, and another sign of the wealth of material lurking here, is the figure of the shambling, ribald skivvy from the café where Morris hangs out. He thinks of her as the Struldbrug – the name given in Swift's *Gulliver's Travels* to the nightmare immortals who cannot die, but simply get older and older, uglier and uglier. She becomes a motherly presence in his life; indeed, he imagines that perhaps she *is* his mother, who vanished under a bombed building during the war. The Struldbrug is a squatter in the house of shadows, and, on the night of the dance with Honey, Morris thinks they have frightened her to death. But she is a survivor too, and pops up singing her old songs the next morning in the café. So relieved is Morris that for a moment it looks as though we will have a happy ending. The whole cityscape is radiant with a new lease of life: 'He went out into the street, dazed. The street beamed in the arse-end of summer and the women who passed him were beautiful and the men distinguished and even the dogs were interesting' (SD 153).

Honey has already killed Ghislaine, however, so this is a false dawn. None the less, it signals the carnivalesque sensibility that was to triumph in Carter's third book, *Several Perceptions* (1968), and to dominate her last novels. The description of the transformation of the café food is particularly marvellous and funny: 'Deep notes of joy rang from the cream horns ... ham rolls bounded like ecstatic piglets from their Cellophane pens' (*SD* 152). This cheerful magic lacks power to reroute the death-directed plot, and the maternal Struldbrug, likewise, remains a minor character. However, such symbolic gestures enrich the novel and lend ambiguity to its author's love-affair with dandyism and despair.

*The Magic Toyshop* simplifies things wonderfully. It is deservedly the most popular of the early novels, a classic rite-of-passage book which contrives to orphan its heroine Melanie twice over, once from her middle-class 'real' family, and a second time from her ogre uncle, Philip Flower. He is a parody-patriarch who rules over the same sort of shadow world that ate up Ghislaine, Honey, and Morris in Carter's first book, and adolescent Melanie finds herself in his power as a result of stepping over the boundary between reality and fantasy. One moonlit night she tries on her mother's wedding-dress and — as if by horrible sympathetic magic – her parents are killed in a plane crash on the other side of the Atlantic.

This 'wedding-dress night, when she married the shadows' (*MT* 77), exiles her and her younger brother and sister from their comfortable, liberal, middle-class home in the country, to live in a dark, narrow house above Uncle Philip's toyshop in south London. They exchange prosperity for poverty, country for city, the indulgent present for the authoritarian past, and – most important – a world of common-sense realism for one which works according to the laws of dreams, fairytales, folktales, myth, and magic. Aunt Margaret, they are told, was struck dumb on the day she married Uncle Philip; she and her two brothers, Francie and Finn Jowle, were orphans themselves, and are unwilling Irish captives in the toyshop. Uncle Philip has made images of them as toy monkeys, they are in his power, and now Melanie, Jonathan, and Victoria join them in this house where there are no mirrors and no books, *because it is the world you find in books and mirrors*, the region of copies and images and representations.

So humans, animals, and toys inhabit the same dimension in this text. Uncle Philip specializes in kitsch artefacts which deliberately insult both 'life' and 'art' by mixing up the two, like the scary jack-in-the-box he once sent Melanie – 'a grotesque caricature of her own face leered from the head that leapt out at her' (*MT* 12) – or the toyshop cuckoo clock which houses 'a real

15

cuckoo, stuffed, with the sounding mechanism trapped, some-how, in its feathered breast' (*MT* 60). Melanie feels 'withered and diminished' when she contemplates the cuckoo, a very mild foretaste of her humiliation and terror when Uncle Philip recruits her to play the part of Leda and be 'raped' by his huge puppet swan. In 'Flower's Puppet Microcosm' flesh and wood, images and originals, share a sinister equality: ' "He's pulled our strings" ', says Finn (*MT* 152). All the same, this cruel factory of simulacra is where you find yourself.

Plunged into want and fear and dirt and dreams, Melanie avoids the bright bourgeois future that was in store for her, and is initiated into the uses of magic. She might, we're told, have grown up to be like the silly 'expensive woman' who comes into the shop looking for ' "something little and gay" ' – 'the sort of woman who used to come for the weekend at home ... with a suitcase full of little black dresses for cocktails and dinner' (*MT* 95–6). Instead she is drawn into the Jowles' occult rebellion, conducted through music, images, and incest. She learns to dream prophetically. She rescues her brother Jonathan from the fire that consumes the shop by dreaming him in advance into the scenery of Uncle Philip's stage, 'the painted water ... swirled and splashed.... The ship was ready to sail away' (*MT* 176). And she herself survives to start the world with smelly and sensuous Finn – both of them subject to a sudden vertigo and uncertainty now that the old man has been dethroned.

*The Magic Toyshop* goes further towards explaining the past's meanings for Carter: like Alice in Lewis Carroll's *Alice through the Looking Glass*, Melanie has to walk in the opposite direction if she wants to get ahead. Despite appearances, the past is the nearest route to the future. In her next novel, *Several Perceptions*, this back-to-the-future plot is handled in a superficially more realistic fashion. However, the central character Joseph (Carter 'identified' alternately with male and female characters during the 1960s) is named after the biblical dreamer, and takes his surname (Harker) from the narrator of Bram Stoker's *Dracula*, so that appearances are yet again deceptive. Beginning with ends, too, is getting to be a habit, for Joseph attempts suicide very shortly after this book's opening, and the remaining action is about his making a reluctant truce with life. He is hopelessly disoriented, unstuck in time, and the book mimics his condition with its picture of a desultory, shiftless world in which hippies and vagrants, tramps and a whore whose family were 'fairground people' (*SP* 122), form a drifting counter-culture. This motley company is united at a Christmas party, given by the book's androgynous master of ceremonies, Kay, in his dying mother's decaying mansion, a 'mausoleum ... full of tatty splendour' (*SP* 11), where various unholy miracles take place. Anne Blossom, an 'iron flower' (*SP* 128), rigid with guilt and repression, loses her limp and learns to dance, Joseph's cat produces a litter of snow-white kittens, the whole cast form for a moment a commune or *endless* family. Hierarchy and coupledom are suspended. In short, it's a benevolent variation on the puppet-master theme, good magic in the foreground: a world where '"Father is only a hypothesis"' (*SP* 121; this line is used again in *Wise Children* (1991), a further example of the persistence of Carter's themes, and the kinship between this early novel and her last carnivalesque books). According to the first edition *Several Perceptions* was written fast, between March and December 1967, and it is rather like a Christmas present, a fable of innocence regained: 'It was the time of the winter solstice, one of the numinous hinges of the year' (*SP* 149).

Starting with ends, ending with beginnings, the Angela Carter of the 1960s was experimenting with different ways of opening up her texts. As I wrote in *Women in the House of Fiction*: 'There's a recurrent Carter plot from these years which, if you translated it into more or less realistic terms, would go like this: a middle-class virgin bewitched and appalled by the fictions of femininity falls in love with a working-class boy, a dandified, dressed-up tramp who's meant to make sense of her desires, but doesn't.' However, the material is not represented in a realist way, in steady, middle-distance focus. In *Several Perceptions*, for instance, this part of the plot has happened before the book begins, for Joseph's ex-lover Charlotte has left him six months before, 'continuing her search for real people' (*SP* 116) elsewhere. What applies to people and plot applies to settings as well. Carter concentrates on the decay of houses, and municipal parks and gardens, to the point where you can glimpse a shamelessly symbolic setting – the Gothic mansion, the weedy Eden of paradise lost.

*Heroes and Villains* (1969) takes off into this future of ruins, by employing the familiar science-fiction convention of the world after the Bomb. This time – continuing Carter's habit of alternating

17

genders – the narrative is done from the point of view of Marianne, who runs away from the white tower where she grew up with her Professor-father. Professors live in orderly communities mostly made up of craftsmen and farmers, guarded by soldiers. Outside there are forests and the ruins of cities, inhabited by shapeless mutants and tribes of wandering Barbarians who raid Professor-villages from time to time, and who have haunted Marianne's dreams ever since she watched one of them kill her brother when she was 10. All of which is partly mocking code for the mental landscape of a late 1960s woman intellectual – the glamour of the guerilla underground and various vagrant counter-cultural movements, the siege of university campuses, etcetera. The tattooed and painted barbarians, 'dressed in furs and brilliant rags' (HV 4) are fashionable dandies, and their shaman Donally is a drop-out Professor in the manner of Timothy Leary. Much more important than such topical allegory, however, is the novel's sceptical exploration of the whole mystique of Otherness.

It is one thing, Carter seems to be saying, to demolish the bourgeois security of family and home, and to get out from under the power of the patriarch, but it is quite another to escape the bad magic of mythologies. We mythologize Nature and Sex as 'outside' history, but they are not. Marianne's fascination with Jewel, the painted archetype who murdered her brother, is gradually complicated by furious disappointment, pain, and (even) pity, once she joins the wanderers. The image-repertoire of *Heroes and Villains* – the puppet-master, the dark house, the sinister wedding-dress, the fire – is recognizably that of *The Magic Toyshop*, but here the images are put to work much more deliberately, and questioned much more thoroughly. One of the book's most impressive achievements is to give the landscape of fantasy its full due of ambivalence. The vertiginous uncertainty of the earlier novel's ending, with girl and boy on the brink of an unknowable future, is the dominant feeling throughout the narrative.

In fact, it is a text that specializes in liminal pleasures – pleasures of the threshold, the mix of dread and bliss that comes from being poised on the edge of extinction. The turret room, up the rotted spiral stair, where Marianne and Jewel bed together (for instance), provides a near-perfect setting for such sensations: shaken by the winds, half-roofless, with the night sky as ceiling and a holly-bush growing in the corner. This decaying house that is opening up to the elements invites creative vandalism, and it's no surprise that almost the only unanimous act that Marianne and Jewel perform is to burn it down:

> In a few moments, the gilded cherubim were blazing cheerfully. Jewel and Marianne, united in a joint purpose, retreated to the doorway and watched the chapel consume itself.... Within the twinkling of an eye, the eclectic façade was consumed and the internal structure of the house revealed, ablaze, caging an intense white core which radiated red, yellow and mauve flames. (*HV* 98–9)

They start with the chapel which Donally, playing God, inhabited. They are behaving like deconstructionists, agents of impatient scepticism who are bent on rendering transparent the prisons of tradition and myth we inhabit. Jewel is an intellectual of sorts, too, as it turns out – not at all the noble savage or glamourous barbarian or perfect Other. And so (with a characteristic Carter irony) he too suffers from self-consciousness and lack of conviction. His acts of destruction and iconoclasm are no more pure than hers.

The result, for the reader, is a curious double-take: at first sight there is the appeal of romance (wilderness, the demon lover); on second thoughts there is the more complex but equally exhilarating sensation of recognizing that the binary oppositions (inside/ outside, culture/nature, masculine/feminine) are themselves being called into question. The roles the characters play are ambivalent. Though Jewel is the rapist, he is also the sex-object and victim. Donally has tattooed an Adam and Eve tableau on Jewel's beautiful back: ' "He might even make me up into a ceremonial robe and wear me on special occasions" ' (*HV* 86). And though Marianne is the victim, she is also the puppet-master's successor: ' "What I'd like best," ' she says to Jewel, ' "would be to keep you in preserving fluid in a huge jar on the mantelpiece in my peaceful room" ' (*HV* 137). Such Gothic cruelties take on a new meaning here – they are metaphors for human alienation in a world where you recognize your own artificiality, your own constructedness. 'I can date to that time ... and to the sense of heightened awareness of the society around me in the summer of 1968, my own questioning of the nature of my reality as a *woman*.' One of the most telling and ironic moments in *Heroes and Villains* occurs in the book's closing scene on the sea-shore, where a pregnant Marianne contemplates her future role in the tribe: ' "I'll be the tiger lady and rule them with a rod of iron" ' (*HV* 150). Mythology rules once more – matriarchy instead of patriarchy, but the winner is the old habit of mind: as critic Gerardine Meaney says in *(Un)Like Subjects*, 'If a woman takes time off from thinking, it seems she's in danger of becoming a mother goddess.'[7]

There are two things about *Heroes and Villains* that mark the development of Carter's cunning: first, the rigorous quality of the fantasy, her insistence on thinking her way through the romance of exclusion: and, secondly, the use she makes of pre-novelistic narrative strategies, particularly the picaresque, with its wandering serial formula, ideal for picturing movement with no definitive goal or end. This was to become the narrative mode of her speculative novels in the next decade (it appealed to her also as a down-market manner, a tribute to popular fiction). In the meantime, however, she rounded out the 1960s with an extraordinary elegy for utopia, *Love* – not published until 1971, but written in 1969. It is a bitterly perfect book, a bleak celebration of the emptiness you arrive at if you rubbish the real too thoroughly. In a sense it's a rewrite of *Shadow Dance*, with the shadows (images, unrealities) taking over yet again. Glamorous, sinister Honeybuzzard from her first book has been split into two, the 'Honey' reborn as beautiful Lee, the Buzzard as Buzz, his dark half-brother. The girl who is their go-between ends up as a blasphemous sacrifice to fantasies of power in both books – though Ghislaine is murdered, and Annabel in *Love* kills herself, the difference is not so great as it sounds, since both girls die of delusion, overdosed on role-playing, and complicit in their own destruction.

There is no patriarch or puppet-master character in *Love*, however. The text's propensity for violence is distributed amongst the three central figures, who form a lethal love–hate triangle. The half-brothers are orphaned sons of a mad mother, rootless products of a lost working-class culture, Annabel is a middle-class drop-out, and they meet in the new no-man's land of Sixties Bohemia, where they proceed to mutilate and misread each other. The writing has a beauty — a glowing patina of craft and indifference – that exactly fits the artificial 'nature' of the people: Annabel's craziness and second-hand Art School images; Buzz's alienated, jealous insistence on seeing everything through a camera lens; Lee's goodness which is really self-love, his niceness which is perhaps merely a chronic eye infection that makes him weep easy tears. Lee is the failed folk-hero, a handsome, confident Jack-the-lad who finds himself lost in the fun-house. Annabel and Buzz both desire him, and conspire with each other against him, leeching away his anyway shaky sense of identity. Or that is one way of looking at it. The narrative point of view is Lee's more than anyone else's, but, given the coolness of the tone, that isn't saying a great deal. Once upon a time Lee would have delivered sexual redemption, now he does not. Sex is turning out to be an exercise in alienation, not the stuff of revelation and intimacy. Bodies have lost the innocence and materiality we used to attribute to them, and flesh has revealed itself as culturally conditioned, a kind of costume or disguise.

So one of the novel's crueller structural refinements (again reminiscent of *Shadow Dance*) is that Lee is allowed a brief midsummer night's idyll with earthy, street-wise Joanne at the very same time that vampire Annabel is slipping into her coma. There is a glimpse of a happy ending – a loose end, an open door – except that we already know (though he does not) the guilty truth. The writing takes on an air of conscious unreality, dramatic irony, the poignancy of paradise lost:

> The silver-plated trees cast barely visible shadows on the grass and each blade and daisy, each bud and blossom, shone with an individual, clear, distinct brilliance. The south side of the park was far more luxuriantly wooded than the north and the man and his girl stepped off the path and walked through the moist undergrowth between the bleached trunks of trees, in and out of the stippled light, until they glimpsed before them the serene white pillars of the miniature temple. All was calm, all was bright. The pale light magically rendered Joanne's gaudy dress as a brief tunic of vague, leopard-like blotches and a few twigs and leaves caught in her hair. (*L.* 121–2)

Lee and Joanne simply cannot sustain the classic, timeless simplicity of 'the man and his girl' (' "Sweet Jesus," thought Lee, "I've knocked off one of my fifth form" ' (*L.* 123)) and in any case dead Annabel has taken possession of the final scene – 'a painted doll, bluish at the extremities.... Flies already clustered round her eyes' (*L.* 124). This is Carter's Camp triumph, experience transformed into theatre, with nearly nothing left over once the curtain falls.

Rounding off her first decade as a writer, Carter had circled back on herself. Marc O'Day calls *Shadow Dance, Several Perceptions*, and *Love* her Bristol trilogy, and certainly grouping the three novels together makes sense.[8] They share a stylized but none the less recognizably contemporary setting, they quote and borrow and beg and steal, they are half in love with death, and derive an indecent energy from the images of decay and boredom and disillusion. They are, as O'Day argues, in a sense realist texts – except that you have to remember that reality has been infiltrated by fiction, so that these novels that represent it have the extra density of fiction squared. She had already plotted her path out of this kind of book in the speculative works: ends could also be beginnings. Underlining the point, she revisited and revised *Love*, in fact, years later (1987), teasing out futures for the surviving characters in an Afterword, looking back mock-scandalized at her 'almost sinister feat of male impersonation' with Lee (*LO* 113) and congratulating herself on having – in the case of Buzz – prophesied the coming of punk. For Annabel, of course, she could do nothing – the book remained 'Annabel's coffin' (*LO* 114), a polished box lined with mirror-glass, Carter's farewell to the Sixties.

'Perhaps in the beginning, there was a curious room.' Crammed with wonders? The beginning, for Carter, is a magical lumber-room. Over the years her own south London house came rather to resemble this cabinet of curiosities. It was a toy-box long before her son Alexander arrived, though he completed its transformation, so that there was hardly room to swing a cat. Indeed, the cats were eventually exiled to the garden. A letter she wrote to me just after that first 1977 interview records the beginnings of this process:

> The *New Review* piece is smashing. Thanks. The only snag, as far as I'm concerned, is that I only have the one script, alas, so that a number of the details of my autobiography are repeated in the 'Family Life' piece – repeated word for word, what's more. Which is a great tribute to my internal consistency, I suppose; only, my childhood, boyhood and youth is a kind of cabaret turn performed, nowadays, with such a practised style it comes out engine-turned on demand. What a creep I am.
>
> And I always get cast down by my own pusillanimity. The notion that one day the red dawn will indeed break over Clapham is the one thing that keeps me going. Of course, I have my own private lists prepared for the purges but.... I'm more interested in socialist reconstruction *after*

the revolution than the revolution itself, which seems to mark me out from my peers. We have just had the exterior of this house painted quite a jolly red, by the way. The front steps look as if the Valentine's day massacre had been performed on them. However, I also managed to persuade Christine downstairs to have a *black* front door so it is the jolly old red & black & VIVA LA MUERTE & sucks boo to Snoo's barley and bamboos; we're going to have a real Clapham front garden, the anarchist colours & pieces of motorcycle & broken bottles & used condoms lightly scattered over all....

P.S. I didn't manage to post this until today, Sunday, or rather 00.30 Monday morning, after a brisk search for the letter (in Portuguese) inviting me to this ruddy do [a festival of Free Art], which begins to look more and more like a nightmare. Chris wants me to bring home a 6 ft. ceramic cockerel. I have house-guests, just arrived, having driven from Nepal – the sister of a Korean ex-boyfriend of mine plus her bloke. Mark has strained a muscle in his back – I'd planned to have him push me around in my wheelchair in 20 years time; what if I have to push him around in one in 5 years time? It is like a soap opera in this house, an everyday story of alternative folk, I suppose.

You can see in the discussion of the décor here something of her inverted dandyism; also the self-consciousness which was her inalienable inheritance, for better and for worse.

# 2

# Middle

they seemed to have made the entire city into a cold hall of mirrors
which continually proliferated whole galleries of constantly changing
appearances, all marvellous but none tangible.... One morning, we
woke to find the house next door reduced to nothing but a heap of
sticks and a pile of newspapers neatly tied with string, left out for the
garbage collector.

Angela Carter, 'A Souvenir of Japan'[1]

Japan (1969–72) had been her rite of passage in between: 'In 1969,
I was given some money to run away with, and did so. The
money was the Somerset Maugham Travel Award and five
hundred pounds went further in those days; it took me as far as
Japan....' (*NS* 28). This was the place where she lost and found
herself. Being young was traumatic; she had been anorexic, her
tall, big-boned body and her intransigent spirit had been at odds
with the ways women were expected to be, inside or outside.
Looking back to her teenage years, she always made the same
joke: 'I now [1983] recall this period with intense embarrassment,
because my parents' concern to protect me from predatory boys
was only equalled by the enthusiasm with which the boys I did
indeed occasionally meet protected themselves against me' (*F.* 23).
Years later, when she became a great admirer of the brilliant and
long-neglected Australian writer Christina Stead, she was to
recognize a kindred spirit, another love-adventuress baffled by
male inhibitions. (In Hazel Rowley's biography we learn that
Stead long remembered the way she would call out to the boys, as
a little girl, 'the boys who did not answer'.[2]) Angela Carter
portrayed her own first marriage as a more or less desperate
measure, with her making the running ('somebody who would go
to Godard movies with me and on CND marches and even have
sexual intercourse with me, though he insisted we should be

engaged first' (*F.* 23) ). And in her five 1960s novels the point of view is interestingly vagrant – as readily 'male' as 'female', as we have seen.

When she impersonated a girl, she described the boys as sex objects; when she went in for cross-dressing, she did it, she later remarked, with almost 'sinister' effectiveness: 'I was, as a girl, suffering a degree of colonialisation of the mind. Especially in the journalism I was writing then, I'd – quite unconsciously – posit a male point of view as the general one. So there was an element of the male impersonator about this young person as she was finding herself' (NFL 71). She adopted the supposedly male point of view also because, under the mask of the 'general', it was more aggressive, more licensed, more geared to *wanting*, more *authorial*. At any rate, the result is that in the early fiction her boys and girls look into each others' eyes and see – themselves:

> I find it very odd [she wrote in 1988] that women who are otherwise perfectly sensible say that the 'sexual revolution' of the sixties only succeeded in putting more women on the sexual market for the pleasure of men. What an odd way of looking at it. This seems to deny the possibility of sexual pleasure to women except in situations where it's so edged around with qualifications that you might as well say, like my mother used to say, 'Don't do it until you've got the ring on your finger....'
>
> Sexual pleasure was suddenly divorced from not only reproduction but also status, security, all the foul traps men lay for women in order to trap them into permanent relationships. Sex as a medium of pleasure....
>
> But then, again, there's no such thing as a pure pleasure and if the relations between men and women were simplified ... by changes in sexual behaviour ... then in other ways they became much, much more complex. Women tend to be raised with a monolithic notion of 'maleness', just as men are raised with the idea of a single and undifferentiated femininity. Stereotyping. (YO 214)

This long quotation is a useful reminder of the ambivalence of her experience of Sixties 'liberation', and her refusal to join in the later chorus of disillusion. For her the Sixties were the period when the illusions broke, dissolved, came out in their true colours: 'towards the end of the sixties it started to feel like living on a demolition site – one felt one was living on the edge of the unimaginable' (YO 211). In 1969, in the course of writing *Love*, she broke the pattern of her own life. She and her husband parted company, and she went to live with a Japanese lover, in Japan. And there her size – and her colour – made her utterly foreign. She compounded her oddity when she stepped into the looking-glass world of a culture that reflected her back to herself as an alien, 'learning the hard way that most people on this planet are *not* Caucasian and have no reason to either love or respect Caucasians'. Her 1974 collection, *Fireworks*, contains three stories that, most uncharacteristically, are hardly fictionalized at all. She must have felt that their built-in strangeness provided sufficient distance, and it does:

> I had never been so absolutely the mysterious other. I had become a kind of phoenix, a fabulous beast; I was an outlandish jewel. He found me, I think, inexpressibly exotic. But I often felt like a female impersonator.
>
> In the department store there was a rack of dresses labelled: 'For Young and Cute Girls Only'. When I looked at them, I felt as gross as Glumdalclitch. I wore men's sandals ... the largest size. My pink cheeks, blue eyes and blatant yellow hair made of me, in the visual orchestration of this city ... an instrument which played upon an alien scale. ... He was so delicately put together that I thought his skeleton must have the airy elegance of a bird's and I was sometimes afraid that I might smash him. (FW 7)

Feeling a freak (Glumdalclitch is the kindly giantess from Book Two of Swift's *Gulliver's Travels*) was a kind of rehearsal for the invention of her lumpen winged aerealiste Fevvers years later. At the time, in Tokyo, whatever she was looking for, she found out the truthfulness *and finality* of appearances, images emptied of their usual freight of recognition and guilt. This was not, in other words, old-fashioned orientalism, but the new-fangled sort that denied you access to any *essence* of otherness. I have already invoked Roland Barthes once, and he comes in again here too. His 1970 book on Japan, *Empire of Signs*, demonstrates the sort of thing that smart semioticians secretly wanted at the time – to discover a culture that despised depth, where 'the inside no longer commands the outside'.[3] The strange tongue

> constitutes a delicious protection ... an auditory film which halts at his ears all the alienations of the mother tongue: the regional and social origins of whoever is speaking, his degree of culture, of intelligence, of taste. ... The unknown language ... forms around me, as I move, a

faint vertigo, sweeping me into its artificial emptiness, which is consummated only for me: I live in the interstice, delivered from any fulfilled meaning.[4]

In other words (Barthes doesn't exactly say this, of course) you can escape your culture's sexual norms, and feel free to sleep with strangers: 'in Japan the body exists, acts, shows itself, gives itself, without hysteria, without narcissism, but according to a pure – though subtly discontinuous – erotic project.'[5] Tokyo is a cruel, delightful mirror to the occidental. The coincidence between Barthes's Japan and Carter's is striking: they visited the same country of the skin, no question, and its topography derives from their very Western wants.

Witness Angela's *Fireworks* story called 'Flesh and the Mirror', about sex minus words, class, character, with a wandering stranger, in 'an unambiguous hotel with mirror on the ceiling' (*FW* 63–4): 'I was the subject of the sentence written on the mirror.... Nothing kept me from the fact, the act; I had been precipitated into knowledge of the real conditions of living' (*FW* 65). Like Barthes, she treasures the new sense she has of the resistance of surfaces. In the Western world 'Women and mirrors are in complicity with one another to evade the action I/she performs that she/I cannot watch, the action with which I break out of the mirror, with which I assume my appearance. But *this* mirror refused to conspire with me; it was like the first mirror I'd even seen' (*FW* 65). This I/she is purely impersonal, has for a moment no biological destiny at all. She discards her inner life and her act delivers her back to herself, her own author. With this vertiginous experience Carter seems to have exorcized her fear of freakishness and made it writable. The whole episode may of course have been a fantasy bred out of the city. But I think it probably did happen: we expect autobiographical writing to belong to the confiding, realist mode, and this does not; it looks like an 'exercise' in literary gymnastics. That, though, does not make it out of character for Carter, who was becoming more and more openly obsessed with the notion that what we accept as natural is the product of a particular history. Art's purpose on this view is to help us recognize our own artificiality – compare the way toys and people intermingle in her fiction – and to estrange us from our home-selves.

Among the journalistic pieces she wrote from Japan for *New*

*Society* is one on tattooing (*irezumi*). This writing on the body already fascinated her; Jewel in *Heroes and Villains* has the Genesis tableau on his back; Annabel in *Love* takes guilty Lee to have a heart tattooed on his chest, her signature, so that he must wear his love on the outside. Annabel chooses green, the most painful colour. In Japan, the pain of the tattoo is ritualized, elaborated, and multiplied: 'It transforms its victim into a genre masterpiece.... he exudes the weird glamour of masochism.... The puppets of the Bunraku theatre are the most passionate in the world; *ikebana* is the art of torturing flowers. *Irezumi* paints with pain on a canvas of flesh' (*NS* 33). The whole process, which she describes in charming and chilling detail, again exemplifies the culture of surfaces: 'In Japan, the essence is often the appearance' (*NS* 36). However, it is striking that, despite the cultural common ground she shares with Barthes, her understanding of all this lets in (as his does not) pain, and the drama of sado-masochism. 'And though it is difficult to ascertain the significance of *irezumi*, it is almost certainly one of the most exquisitely refined and skilful forms of sado-masochism the mind of man ever divined,' she writes (*NS* 38). Barthes would have stopped at the intersticial bliss of failing to ascertain the significance, rather as he stopped short of openly declaring his homosexuality. Carter's feminist politics of the flesh became explicit. 'In Japan', she said, looking back, 'I learnt what it was to be a woman and became radicalised' (*NS* 28).

Self-consciousness had been her bane from the start, hence the anorexia. But, while most women come out the other side and learn to act naturally, she managed not to, and Japan is the shorthand, I think, for how. She discovered and retained a way of looking at herself, and other people, as unnatural. She was, even in ordinary and relaxed situations, a touch unlikely on principle. Her hair went through all the colours of the rainbow, before becoming white at the moment when decorum would have suggested a discreet, still-youthful streaked mouse. Once when I was staying at her house I discovered I had mislaid my make-up, and she dug out a paint-box from Japan, some kind of actor's or geisha's kit, which was all slick purple, rusty carmine, and green grease.

She escaped the character expected of the woman writer by similar strategies. That is, she substituted work for inwardness. She had once wanted, in adolescence, to be an actress; when I talked with her in 1977, she insisted that writing was *public*: 'Sometimes when you say to people you're a writer, they say, "Have you had anything published?" Which is a bit like saying to an actor, "Have you ever been on the stage?" Because if it's not published it doesn't exist.' And the same point, made more succinctly: 'I mean, it's like the right, true end of love' (SS 54–5). She was – as so often – quoting, in this case the opening lines from one of the most bawdy and cynical of Donne's 'Elegies' (number XVIII):

> Who ever loves, if he do not propose
> The right true end of love, he's one that goes
> To sea for nothing but to make him sick....

Donne's poetry had been in the 1950s on all the reading lists. He was a mainstay of literary (and heterosexual) values, someone who stood for the redeeming power of passionate love. Carter makes characteristically ironic use of this fact, in the last scenes of *The Magic Toyshop*: 'John Donne, 1572–1632.... In the school poetry book.... How all the young girls loved John Donne' (*MT* 193). *Her* version of Donne was a dandy and an actor, not the touchstone of sincerity. The quotation from Elegy XVIII is all about the *act* of love/sex, not the inner state of being in love. She had turned Donne round into a fellow de-mystifier.

Carter, like every writer, needed to find and/or create a background out of the stuff of her own culture. Japan confirmed her in her sense of strangeness, but it was the impetus she had built up through her own early work that had sent her on her travels, after all. Plus her reading – Swift's *Gulliver's Travels*, the antinomian, visionary poetry (and etchings) of William Blake, Lewis Carroll's *Alice* books, for instance. Plus medieval romances, read at university, plus French symbolists, decadents, and Dadaists. She picked and chose her literary parents, and in that she was very much in the teasing about-to-be-mainstream of European writing – along with (for example) Vladimir Nabokov (also obsessed with Alice), whose *Lolita* (1956) was the Camp masterpiece of its decade. Nabokov's stylish, rootless, and insidious narrator Humbert Humbert quoted continuously – Carroll, Poe, Pushkin, Baudelaire, Shakespeare.... He was the very type of European culture in its dissolving or deconstructive phase. 'I've just been offered a teaching job in Minnesota,' Carter wrote in a 1977 letter; 'am very torn about it, don't know what to do ... I don't fine [sic] the intellectual climate in Britain all that stimulating, oh, no, indeed; but I felt like Humbert Humbert when I went to America for a holiday, once, a crumbling relic of European decadence stranded among the babes in the wood.' Her attitude to the United States was to undergo radical changes, but her jokey reference to 'a crumbling relic of European decadence' was true enough to her shadowy, self-conscious Gothic heritage. Closer to home, as with Donne, she was mocking even where she admired. D. H. Lawrence's social world she recognized up to a point in her grandmother's, but she was inevitably resistant to his bullying on behalf of phallic wisdom. The trial and subsequent publication of the unexpurgated version of *Lady Chatterley's Lover* had been one of the great literary events of the 1960s: a libertarian victory on behalf of a profoundly reactionary text, which set out to police the boundaries separating male and female, disturbed (for Lawrence's generation) by the arrival of the Edwardian New Woman. Lawrence became a critical battleground for the new feminists and their enemies: Kate Millett in *Sexual Politics* (1970) plotted out his murderous misogyny; Norman Mailer in *The Prisoner of Sex* (1971) praised him as 'the sacramental poet of a sacramental act'.[6] Angela Carter's contribution to the polemical dossier on Lawrence and sexuality was characteristically wicked and witty – 'Lorenzo the Closet-queen' (1975), 'a brief, sartorial critique of *Women in Love'* (*NS* 162), which reveals him as an authorial cross-dresser, a fetishist of femininity:

> Like a drag-queen, but without the tragic heroism that enables a transvestite to test the magic himself, he believes women's clothes are themselves magical objects which define and confine women.... The con trick, the brilliant, the wonderful con trick, the real miracle, is that his version of drag has been accepted as the real thing. (*NS* 167–8)

The bawdy and disrespectful humour of this brief essay was one of *her* main weapons in the sexual-politics war. Here, she pulls canonized Lawrence back into the ranks of the ambivalent. He reminds her of the *onnegata*, the male actors who play women in kabuki theatre in Japan. Her spell on the other side of the world helped her to recognize the strangeness of back home.

Not that she stopped consulting the mirror. A small allegory: Plotinus and later Neo-platonists suggested mischievously that you could draw a subversive moral from the fate of Narcissus – it is not self-obsession that destroys you, but the failure to love yourself coolly and intelligently and sceptically enough. If he'd recognized his own image in the water, he could have made a real beginning on knowing himself. Carter made much the same point, looking back on the Sixties, and quoting one of William Blake's *Proverbs of Hell*: ' "If the fool persists in his folly, he becomes wise." ' I suppose that was how I came to feminism, in the end, because still and all there remained something out of joint and it turned out that was it, rather an important thing, that all the time I thought things were going so well I was a second class citizen' (YO 215). Persisting in her folly meant stepping into the looking-glass, not away from it. And she would look into some dangerous mirrors – like de Sade's (in *The Sadeian Woman* (1979) ), but by then she had stepped through Japanese reflections, and could say – for example – 'Flesh comes to us out of history' (*SW* 11). 'Someday,' wrote Barthes in *Empire of Signs*, 'we must write the history of our own obscurity – manifest the density of our narcissism.'[7]

When Angela Carter came back to England, she had her career to build all over again, and that is what she did, with help from journalism (*New Society* and the *Guardian*), an Arts Council Fellowship in Sheffield (1976–8), and so forth. She was hard up, and marginalized in ways she did not relish at all. She had no secure relationship with a publisher – between 1971 and 1977 she moved from Hart-Davis to Quartet to Gollancz – she couldn't make enough money out of her fiction to live on, and she didn't fit easily into the classic outsider role. She never accepted the madwoman-in-the-attic school of thought about the woman writer, particularly not about the Gothic or fantastical writer: freaks and fairies, she believed, were as much socially determined as anyone else, our 'symbols' are of course *ours*. Theory apart, however, she had a thin time during the 1970s, and she was painfully prickly about reputations. When she filled in an author's publicity form for Gollancz, who published *The Passion of New Eve* in 1977, there was a section asking her to list her previous publications. Angela wrote simply '7 novels', without giving even the titles. In a letter at the time she worried about being ghettoized as fantastical: 'I suspect Golly's have buggered it by inventing a new category – Gollancz Fantasy and the Macabre [sic] – for it; it seemed a good idea at the time but may precipitate the novel into a reviewer's limbo. It is also a very evil book; I felt white as a lamb after I had laid down my pen, que faire.' She knew all about the reviewer's limbo: the other major speculative novel she had published on her return, *The Infernal Desire Machines of Doctor Hoffman* (1972), had been ignored, or treated with incomprehension and contempt, by most mainstream critics, and *New Eve* met with the same fate. It would take a new kind of publishing context, and a new intellectual climate, to make her allegories of change truly readable.

Shortly before the publication of *New Eve*, she wrote to me from Albert Road, Sheffield, about Virago, and her great friend and fan Carmen Callil's plans to *re*publish women. She was thinking hard about 'the woman writer', and meeting a drunken Elizabeth Smart at a party at Emma Tennant's had given her bitter food for thought:

> 'It is hard for women,' she slurred. Actually, it was a very peculiar experience because she clearly wanted to talk in polished gnomic epigrams about anguish and death and boredom and I honestly couldn't think of anything to say. Except, I understand why men hate women and they are right, yes, right. Because we should set good examples to the poor things. (Was surprised to find Mary Wollstonecraft making exactly the same point, in a way.) ... It was all very odd. I don't mean to sound hard. I mean, I'm sure her life has been astoundingly tragic. And I began to plot a study of the Jean Rhys/E. Smart/E. O'Brien woman titled 'Self-inflicted wounds,' which kind of brings me to the point, or, anyway, a point.
>
> I'm on the editorial committee of this publishing firm, Virago ...

From her point of view, Virago was meant – among many, many other things – to make money out of and for women's writing, and to rescue it from the slough of passive suffering:

> The whole idea is very tentative at the moment, obviously. I suppose I am moved towards it by the desire that no daughter of mine should ever be in a position to be able to write: BY GRAND CENTRAL STATION I SAT DOWN AND WEPT, exquisite prose though it might contain. (BY GRAND CENTRAL STATION I TORE OFF HIS BALLS would be more like it, I should hope.)

She herself was working on the Sade book at the time, and her ideas for Virago included some books by men (Sade's *Justine*, Richardson's *Clarissa*) which got at the roots of female 'pathology'. She feared and loathed and found hilarious the spectacle of the

suffering woman, and her cruelty is a measure of her fear. One of
the images that haunts her fiction, one of her most poignant and
persistent borrowings, is the image of crazy, dying Ophelia, as
described by Gertrude in Shakespeare's *Hamlet*, and (possibly even
more) as painted by Millais: waterlogged, draped in flowers,
drifting downstream to her virgin death. Androgynous Honeybuzzard in *Shadow Dance*, in his madness, is compared to Ophelia –
'His hair trailed like mad Ophelia's and his eyes were too large for
his head.... Under his breath he sang a song they could not hear'
(*SD* 181–2), – and Ophelia is invoked in her last novel, *Wise Children*
(1991), in the story of Tiffany. The drowning mad girl floats along
her narrative streams through the years; no novel is without her
since she is the icon of pathos you must exorcise again and again
and again.

The 1970s novels, *Dr Hoffman* and *New Eve*, are last-days
allegories, reports from the demolition site – 'one was living on
the edge of the unimaginable' – which map out territory for
speculation. *Dr Hoffman* begins in a dissolving city in South
America, where a new kind of civil war has broken out, between
the Reality Principle and the Pleasure Principle. Ordinary life is
being invaded by anarchic images, mocking phantasms and
subversive spooks slither out of the mirrors and out of people's
dreams to usurp the realm of nature and common sense:

> Whether the apparitions were shades of the dead, synthetic
> reconstructions of the living or in no way replicas of anything we
> knew, they inhabited the same dimension as the living ... It was ...
> the heyday of trompe l'œil for painted forms took advantage of the
> liveliness they mimicked. Horses from the pictures of Stubbs in the
> Municipal Art Gallery neighed, tossed their manes and stepped
> delicately off their canvases to go to crop the grass in public parks. A
> plump Bacchus wearing only a few grapes strayed from a Titian into a
> bar and there initiated Dionysiac revelry. (*DRH* 10–13)

South America is very much the right setting for this vertiginous
frontier-crossing – in literary terms, that is. The stories and brief
essays of Argentinian Jorge Luis Borges, collected and translated
into English as *Labyrinths* and *Fictions*, were the advance guard of
an invasion of the English-speaking cultures that became known
as 'magical realism': a way of writing that placed in the same
plane the fantastical and the documentary. Carter had arrived by

her own path in the same strange territory, and in *Dr Hoffman* she was celebrating transatlantic intertextuality. The following passage from another, characteristically eccentric Borges book, *The Book of Imaginary Beings* ('a zoo of mythologies', translated 1969) will serve to show what I mean. Borges, under the heading *Fauna of Mirrors*, is retelling an ancient Cantonese myth:

> In those days the world of mirrors and the world of men were not, as they are now, cut off from each other. They were, besides, quite different; neither beings nor colours, nor shapes were the same. Both kingdoms, the spectacular and the human, lived in harmony; you could come and go through mirrors. One night the mirror people invaded the earth. Their power was great, but at the end of bloody warfare the magic arts of the Yellow Emperor prevailed. He repulsed the invaders, imprisoned them in their mirrors, and forced on them the task of repeating, as though in a kind of dream, all the actions of men.... Nonetheless a day will come when the magic spell will be shaken off.[8]

In fact, this is more or less the plot of *Dr Hoffman* – a precarious victory for the Reality Principle. She referred in a letter to the book's 'dialectic between reason and passion, which it resolves in favour of reason (unlike my life).'

As in *Heroes and Villains*, the narrative is picaresque. This time, however, the 'outsiders' are represented by a whole series of distinct subcultures, from the circus to a tribe of river Indians to a Sadeian brothel peopled with automata and androids to a society of centaurs (related to Swift's Houyhynhmns) to the Gothic castle of the Doctor himself, a kind of giant orgone box where the orchestrator of the Unreal generates his energies out of the secretions of caged lovers. Desiderio begins his travels as a secret agent on behalf of the Real: on his way he falls in love with the Doctor's ambiguous, shape-changing daughter Albertina (named for Proust's ineffable object of desire, who's a boy in disguise), but at the last he discovers with horror, boredom, and desperate regret that the creature he is pursuing is the Doctor's puppet, her father's agent. And so he kills her before she can draw him into the cage, and restores his world to the order of the ordinary once again.... Now Albertina lives on to haunt his dreams, safely and wretchedly locked into the realms of fantasy.

The Doctor is the last and most deadly of Carter's puppet-masters: he is the great patriarchal Forbidder turned Permitter, the one who sets the libido 'free' – a most depressing figure, because he points to the recognition that there's no world *outside* power-games. The last scenes of the story are permeated with pain but also with the dismal *ennui* that comes from recognition: here we are again, back in the Gothic mode, with the mad scientist. There is no sense of triumph at all, of course, only exhaustion, passion (for the moment) spent. One of the most interesting effects of the simple serial structure of picaresque is just this – the generation of a journey that is neither flight nor quest, and of an ending without real closure. Travelling, as the proverb says, is more important than arriving. Indeed, you could say that the main purpose of this wonderful journey is to naturalize writer and reader in the new no man's land of later twentieth-century culture, where no experience comes unmediated, and no pleasure is pure.

*Dr Hoffman* is very much an intellectual's book, for all its seeming simplicity of structure, and its obsessive, erotic, and kinetic images. Its themes would recur as arguments in the Sade study. She needed to *theorize* in order to feel in charge, and to cheer herself up, and that has left its mark marvellously on this 1970s fiction, which is full of ideas, *armed* with them. Desiderio avoids being eaten by the river Indians, who are hoping that way magically to absorb his literacy, because he is a good enough anthropologist to tumble to their plans. Like Angela Carter, he has read his Lévi-Strauss, and though he very much wants to be absorbed in this womb-like family, and luxuriates in 'that slight feeling of warm claustrophobia I had learned to identify with the notion "home"' (*DRH* 83), he proves his separateness by reading their intentions so cleverly. (Much more recently, in *Nights at the Circus* (1984), Fevvers escapes a murderous Rosicrucian by the same ploy, having this time read Frances Yates, I would imagine.)

Another reason for her deepening interest in theory was that 'coming out' as a feminist was hard, even though she had been one in a sense all along. In *The Passion of New Eve* (1977) woman is born out of a man's body once again, as in the Genesis story – an allegory of the painful process by which the 1970s women's movement had had to carve out its own identity from the unisex mould of 1960s radical politics. Men had stood for universality, as Simone de Beauvoir finally came out and said in *All Said and Done* in 1972: 'I thought the state of women and society would evolve together.'[9] But in fact it was with the crisis of notions of evolutionary progress that feminism found a space. *New Eve* moves to North America, a just-future New World where society is breaking down into sects and movements and guerrilla bands, self-fashioning tribes who live according to bizarre codes of their own invention. This America is a wasteland, seeded only with the offspring of disintegration. Not: back to Nature, but: forward to the man-made world. Our myths are part of the picture, and our own identities are thinning out, so that soon (as happens in this 'science-fiction' plot) humans will be able to breed with phantasms.

*New Eve* is a raw and savage book. Carter sacrificed some of her habitual charm when she started to anatomize the androgynous zone she had so far contrived to inhabit. The symbols are *known* as symbols from the start: at the centre of everything is Tristessa, a Hollywood goddess in the Garbo mould, long vanished into seclusion and thus impeccably glamorous, a timeless erotic shimmer on the silver screen: 'Tristessa's speciality had been suffering. Suffering was her vocation. She suffered exquisitely' (*PNE* 8). Bringing this lady of pain back into life and back into question is the aim of the plot – which Carter had anticipated in rather surreal shorthand in a tale called 'Reflections' (*Fireworks*, (1974)). In the story, an ageless hermaphrodite knits a web that keeps the worlds inside and outside the mirror separate, and all hell breaks loose when s/he drops a stitch. In *New Eve* Tristessa, who lives in a glass mausoleum in the desert, and 'sculpts' enormous tear-drops by plopping molten glass into the swimming pool, is the secret centre of mystification. Because she is not a woman at all, it turns out, but (how else could she so perfectly embody the eternal feminine? – 'Her name itself whispered rumours of inexpressible sadness; the lingering sibilants whispered like the doomed petticoats of a young girl who is dying' (*PNE* 122)) an anti-being, the greatest male transvestite of them all.

To this grand unreality Carter mates her 'new Eve', who started off as male Evelyn (a casually sadistic Englishman on his travels) until he was kidnapped and Frankensteinishly remodelled. Mother, the matriarch who does the surgery, reads like an embodiment of an 'old joke of the early sixties' – which Carter recalled in *The Sadeian Woman*: 'The astronaut, returning from heaven, describes God: "This may come as a bit of a shock, but *she's black*" ' (*SW* 110-11). In this narrative mothers and fathers turn up in the most improbable guises. The familiar picaresque plot (one narrow escape after another) has a middle this time, though – an omphalos, a navel, a centrifuge, in the form of Tristessa's shrine. New Eve's alchemical marriage to Tristessa leaves her pregnant on the sea-shore. And we have been here before, not only in the myths, but in Carter's own mythology, in *Heroes and Villains*; however, this time the scene is played through in the eery light of a revisionist dawn. It is hard to put your finger on the difference, exactly. Isn't this just another liminal gesture, poised on the edge? The cave-world Eve explores on this shore, though, gives the refusal to go simply 'Back to Nature' a new twist. Nature gets rewritten.

The newness has two levels – conceptual (a new conception, a brain-child) and stylistic. In her cave Carter unravels the story of evolution, a tale which for so long had wedded the idea of change to the idea of progress, biological destiny, and determinism, the survival of the fittest.... The traditional version of this story said that evolution proceded by selection and diversification, but during the 1970s it was being remapped. (Did she know this? Unlikely: probably both kinds of moves, the games with fiction, and the interrogation of the fossil record, were signs of the times.) As retold by Stephen Jay Gould, in *Wonderful Life* (subtitled *The Burgess Shale and the Nature of History* (1989)), the new evolution-story speaks instead of decimation and stereotyping. By ' "replaying life's tape" ' in imagination, by staging 'the three-dimensional reanimation of squashed and distorted fossils', scientists uncovered a different plot for the record.[10] Not only did they allow themselves to contemplate 'alternative worlds that didn't emerge, but might have arisen', but (says Gould) the new picture provides for a different conception of our humanity – we are creatures with a contingent, fragile provenance: 'we are a thing, an item of history, not an embodiment of general principles.'[11] Going back, you encounter a world of possibilities, in other words.

And in terms of style, well, Carter is becoming more and more convinced that literature has *uses* – that you can use images to deal in ideas, and that the notion that art is serenely separate is a piece of sanitizing piety, designed to keep the creatures of imagination in their cages. ('Fine art, that exists for itself alone, is art in a final state of impotence' (*SW* 13)). The forms that belong to earlier periods before Art for Art's sake interest her ever more intensely, the fairy-tales and allegories and romances; also – the kinds of fiction that are outside the pale of literature, like pornography. She is revising herself, thinking again about her repertoire of obsessive images, and seeing them in a new light. It's a feminist light – though she remains an enemy of the suffering woman (for her this was feminism's *point* in a sense) and chooses as her final 'foremother' figure in *New Eve* this vaudevillian grotesque:

> It was an impressive head. The hair was dyed a brave canary yellow.... All was decorated with peek-a-boo bows of pale pink ribbon.... She wore a two-piece bathing costume in a red and white spotted fabric and, round her shoulders, a stole of glossy and extravagant blond fur but her flesh was wrinkled and ravaged and sagged from her bones. Her face was very dirty but magnificently painted; a fresh coating of white powder and scarlet lipstick and maroon rouge must have been added that very morning.... She sat on her chair and sang of the lights of Broadway, of foggy days in London Town and how she'd learned her lesson but she wished she were in love again.... She wore high-heeled silver sandals on her gnarled old feet and sat facing the ocean like the guardian of the shore. (*PNE* 177)

If this is the Struldbrug from *Shadow Dance*, she's come a long way in the ten years that divide the two books. She has emerged in three dimensions, and full colour, and wears her age with hideous and hilarious confidence. Symbols grow old, and change, too. There is nowhere timeless left, certainly not the womb – the Mother Goddess, duly demoted, waves Eve off to sea, and out of the book: ' "Where can we go, poor things, flotsam of time?" ' (*PNE* 190).

*The Sadeian Woman* strips off the ideas enacted as fiction in *New Eve*, and presents them nakedly as arguments. Sade's pornographic heroines provide Carter with the materials for an ironic exploration of women's plight in a world authorized by patriarchy: 'If women allow themselves to be consoled for their culturally determined lack of access to the modes of intellectual debate by the invocation of hypothetical great goddesses, they are simply flattering themselves into submission....Mother goddesses are just as silly a notion as father gods.' (*SW* 5). The Holy Mother and the suffering daughter are the mythic figures she takes apart, borrowing some of Sade's cruelty to do so. The strategy is to *follow through* the monster Marquis's plots in ironic paraphrase. His perversity spells out the secret subtext of law and order and hierarchy. The style she adopts is full of mock-authority, the mockery of authority, and in this she echoes another of her canonical authors, William Blake and the *Proverbs of Hell*. For example: 'the free expression of desire is as alien to pornography as it is to marriage' (*SW* 13). The central argument, reiterated ruthlessly in many different formulations, is that sexuality must be understood as historical, not timeless or fixed. We must exorcize the 'bankrupt enchantments' and 'fraudulent magic' of myth (*SW* 109). Consolatory fictions must be exposed, and reasoned (and jeered) out of countenance. Women must give up on the eternal feminine, because it leaves them in 'voluntary exile from the historic world, in its historic time that is counted out minute by minute' (*SW* 108).'The goddess is dead.... if the goddess is dead, there is nowhere for eternity to hide. The last resort of homecoming is denied us' (*SW* 110). Carter is so impatiently deconstructive here that there's no room for revisionist perspectives, no rewriting of Nature and evolution. The effect is at once horrid, and bracing (Blake: Damn braces, bless relaxes), a telling reminder, if one were needed, of her dread of passivity.

In the year of *New Eve*, 1977, Carter had also published an elegant translation of *The Fairy Tales of Charles Perrault*; in *The Bloody Chamber* (1979) she produced her own haunting, mocking – sometimes tender – variations on some of the classic motifs of the genre: the Red Riding Hood story, Bluebeard, Sleeping Beauty, Beauty and the Beast. It may seem a project remote from the Sade book, but it was not, for in retelling these tales she was deliberately drawing them out of their set shapes, out of the separate space of 'children's stories' or 'folk art', and into the world of change. It was yet another assault on myth – though this time done caressingly and seductively. The monsters and the princesses lose their places in the old script, and cross the forbidden binary lines. Later she would invoke Jack Zipes's book, *Breaking the Magic Spell: Radical Theories of Folk and Fairy Tales*, also published in 1979, to help explain the special pleasure and suggestiveness you could get out of these transformations. Marxist Zipes argues that 'the best of folk and fairy tales chart ways for us to become masters of history.... they transform time into relative elements'.[12] And he quotes one passage from theoretician Ernst Bloch that fits especially, uncannily, closely with Carter's thinking, and indeed draws together the themes of her 1970s work: 'Humankind still lives in prehistory everywhere, indeed everything awaits the creation of the world as a genuine one. The real genesis is not at the beginning, but at the end, and it only begins when society and existence become radical, that is grasp themselves at the root.'[13] Going back to these preliterary forms of story-telling was 'radical' for her in this sense. She could experiment with her own writer's role, ally herself in imagination with the countless, anonymous narrators who stood behind literary redactors like Perrault or (much later) the brothers Grimm. The experience had a transformational effect on her literary persona – she had emerged (it turned out) from the self-consciousness of the Camp sensibility into a robust political and performative role. She had become a version of the fairy godmother. Though there's continuity there too: for instance, she describes the character of fairy godmothers in Perrault as 'that of women of independent means who've done quite well for themselves ... personages as worldly-wise and self-confident as Mae West' (CP 18–19). Mae West, camp and comic in equal measure, is one of Carter's favourite figures from twentieth-century iconography – her own woman (her own script-writer), large, bawdy, armed with wit against the silver screen's baleful power to make women beautifully pathetic.

So, with the Sade book and *The Bloody Chamber*, she rounded off the decade triumphantly. The fairy-tale idea enabled her to *read* in public with a new appropriateness and panache, as though she was *telling* these stories. She took to teaching creative writing, too. In 1980–1 she went to the States for her first major stint as a teacher, to Brown University, where she substituted for John Hawkes: no one had read her, she said, but she enjoyed it enormously, and had the company of her friends Robert and Pili Coover. Bit by bit, her earlier work would be republished (in Picador and King Penguin, as well as Virago); she would acquire a solid relation with Chatto & Windus, when Carmen Callil moved there; she would become a delighting globe-trotter, a visiting writer/teacher/performer; and her work would be translated into all the major European languages. The point to make about the years in the middle is this: she had to struggle hard to sustain her confidence, in the face of frequent indifference, condescension, and type-casting. She was not, either, able to repose securely in the bosom of the sisterhood, since her insistence on reclaiming the territory of the pornographers – just for example – set her against feminist puritans and separatists. Her later experience in Albany ('upstate New York is *so* beautiful. Rock, & water, & forest') where she taught writing in 1988 was not untypical: 'the only snag is the Women's Studies dept., which is truly terrifying – really hard line radical feminists, who have virtually boycotted me.' And, of course, she was in general an offence to the modest, inward, realist version of the woman writer. John Bayley, in the *New York Review*, reviewing her achievement in retrospect, contrived to imply that she had an almost cosy 'place' from the start: a magical realist, a postmodernist, a politically proper feminist. This could not be further from the truth. Her work was unclassifiable in terms of British fiction, except as 'Gothic' or 'fantasy', throughout the whole difficult middle of her career. If that situation has changed, it is largely because she refused to write 'fantasy' as (merely) alternative, 'in opposition'; and because she made large demands on her readers.

Bad-tempered footnotes department. (Angela Carter was a caustic and far-from-disinterested commentator on the British literary scene. She minded about prizes and reputations, because she minded about reaching readers. Her rude humour sustained her in many a low moment.)

*Exhibit One: A Letter Undated, 'Tuesday'*

> *Very* bland place. At least, Toronto is.... The son and his father didn't miss me. But they seem glad to see me back. It seems we might well be going to Texas next spring; am awaiting letter. Am planning to write novel about sensitive, fine-grained art historian whose [PTO] life is totally changed by winning large, vulgar cash prize, she dies [sic] her hair green and wears leather trousers etc. Sniffs glue and turns into Kathy Acker....

*Exhibit Two: A Postcard from the United States*

> Have just heard about the Booker. I hope he drinks himself to death on the prize money (you know me, ever fair and compassionate). Will telephone soon – I keep meaning to write you the kind of letter people write in biographies, but there ain't time.

# 3

# Ending

> Because I simply could not have existed, as I am, in any other
> preceding time or place.... I could have been a professional writer at
> any period since the seventeenth century in Britain or in France. But I
> could *not* have combined this latter with a life as a sexually active
> woman until the introduction of contraception.... A 'new kind of
> being', unburdened with a past. The voluntarily sterile yet sexually
> active being, existing in more than a few numbers, *is* a being without
> precedent.
>
> Angela Carter, 'Notes from the Front Line'[1]

Angela Carter contributed a story called 'The Quilt Maker' to a
1981 anthology, *Sex and Sensibility*. She was stitching together
autobiography and fiction, and celebrating her return to the house
in south London which – though she left it often – was from now
on her home:

> As you can tell from the colourful scraps of oriental brocade and
> Turkish homespun I have sewn into this bedcover, I then (call me
> Ishmael) wandered about for a while and sowed (or sewed) a wild oat
> or two into this useful domestic article, this product of thrift and
> imagination, with which I hope to cover myself in my old age. (QM 139)

Patchwork, she writes, is a pleasing metaphor for art: 'You can
really make this image work for its living' (QM 122). Art and craft
and the business of being herself came together for her in the
1980s: she taught the craft of writing (Pat Barker, Kazuo Ishiguro,
and Glenn Patterson were among her students in Britain), she
read aloud with increasing pleasure and style, she wrote
introductions, edited anthologies – a Woman of Letters in the
mocking mould of Mother Goose.

The fairy-tale connection was crucial in all this:

> the term 'fairy tale' is a figure of speech and we use it loosely, to

describe the great mass of infinitely various narrative that was, once upon a time and still is, sometimes, passed on and disseminated through the world by word of mouth – stories without known originators that can be remade again and again by every person who tells them.... fairy tales, stories from the oral tradition, are all of them the most vital connection we have with the imaginations of the ordinary men and women whose labour created our world. (*FT*, p.ix)

She enjoyed, too, writing for radio, 'the atavistic lure, the atavistic power, of voices in the dark ... the writer who gives the words to those voices retains some of the authority of the most antique tellers of tales' (*YS* 13). These ongoing experiments with tale-telling models that date from the time before the author was an individual (and usually male) completed her personal transformation of the old 1960s utopian dream of the 'Death of the Author'. *That* had implied, more often than not, a colourless, insubstantial anonymity, the kind of staged *absence* associated with the traditional avant-garde. But the tale-teller's voice is insidious, ribald, thrilling, lying, a role (a presence) that takes you out of yourself:

fairy tales.... are ... anonymous and genderless.... Ours is a highly individualised culture, with a great faith in the work of art as a unique one-off, and the artist as an original, a godlike and inspired creator of unique one-offs. But fairy tales are not like that, nor are their makers. Who first invented meatballs? In what country? Is there a definitive recipe for potato soup? Think in terms of the domestic arts. 'This is how *I* make potato soup.' (*FT*, p.x)

And indeed, the 'I', the first person, becomes more and more prominent in her narratives, although – in accordance with her home-made theory of how a fiction-writer could best confront the late twentieth-century – that 'I' was not exactly *hers*.

She agreed with Christina Stead (who died in 1983 back in her native Australia, finally and grudgingly acknowledged as a major writer) about this, as about much else. 'I love *Ocean of Story*, the name of an Indian treasury of story,' Stead had written in 1968; 'that is the way I think of the short story and what is part of it, the sketch, anecdote, jokes cunning, philosophical, and biting, legends and fragments. Where do they come from? Who invents them? Everyone perhaps.'[2] I mention Stead here because she points up the paradox of this highly idiosyncratic passion for anonymity. Like Carter, Stead was oblique, cussed, bloody-minded (all terms of praise for Carter – see her introduction to

*Wayward Girls and Wicked Women* (1986)). Both of them were originals, and in love with originality – but they refused, stubbornly, to see that as *special*. Back in her first published book, *The Saltzburg Tales* in 1934, one of Stead's spokespersons ('full of tales as the poets of Persia') had argued that 'there must be many ignored talents who have an equal right to fame... I deny the unmistakable hallmark of personality, the unquestionable superiority of everything done by a man of genius.'[3] The notion of the 'genius', the 'godlike and inspired creator', Carter read as a piece of modernist mystification, which made the practitioners of art into a priestly caste, and put about the myth that creativity was *very scarce*. Her chosen myth says the opposite. Like Stead, she was an atheist ('godlike' is emphatically not a term of praise) and a materialist, in art as in life. You had to concoct any separate self, cook one up, cook the books. In 1984, introducing a collection of Stead stories, she wrote that: 'For Stead ... private life is itself a socially determined fiction, the "self" a foetus of autonomy that may or may not prove viable and "inner freedom", far from being an innate quality, is a precariously held intellectual or emotional position'.[4] For Carter, talking about the self as socially determined is liberating: it means that you are part of history, caught up in change. It is from this angle, and with a characteristic mixture of effrontery and modesty, that she describes herself as 'A "new kind of being"', a new kind of woman writer who has been made possible by contraception – able to nourish her 'foetus of autonomy' without giving up on sexual experience. She didn't have to choose between brain-children and children, either: this was a material fact, and one that reduced for her the glamour of the 'godlike' artist, whose romantic agony, etcetera, depended on the great divide between metaphorical making and more literal kinds. So (as in the long ages before literacy) story-telling in our time becomes once more genderless...

This was a utopian fiction, a rival legend to counter the notion of timeless art and godlike artists. In her own stories from the later 1970s and early 1980s collected in *Black Venus* in 1985 she is mischievously engaged in supplementing the canon – writing *round the edges* of the known, resurrecting (by means of invention, naturally) materials that didn't quite make it into the record, and voices we didn't get to hear. She inserts apocryphal episodes into various ready-made traditions – into Baudelaire's biography, and

Poe's (the *real* role of the black Muse, the dead mother's Gothic legacy). The Lizzie Borden murders are set up again behind locked doors, as an anatomy of repression. In 'Our Lady of the Massacre' she composes a first-person adventure Defoe forgot to write up – a Moll Flanders among the Indians. Two of these virtuoso performances (all very different from each other) stand out for me: 'The Kitchen Child' and 'Overture and Incidental Music for *A Midsummer Night's Dream*'. The first is a pastiche folk-tale, in ironical praise of the domestic arts (including the very art of tale-telling we are being treated to). Our narrator, a blithe bastard, is conceived while his enormous mother, the cook, busy whipping up a lobster soufflé, is looking the other way, and he grows up to become the bard of culinary consciousness – the ultimate chef. We are led by the plot to expect a revelation. He is really the heir to an aristocratic fortune, a great name ... but no, he resolutely refuses to recognize his father. The anti-moral is that illegitimacy must be the higher wisdom, since it represents his blissful absorption in his vocation: 'Think in terms of the domestic arts. "This is how *I* make potato soup." '

If 'The Kitchen Child' is a tribute to anonymous creativity, the *Midsummer Night's Dream* story (first published in the science-fiction magazine *Interzone* in 1982) is an irreverent salute to the national Name. Shakespeare's play is subjected to a cunning transformation by means of a sort of pre-script. We are behind the plot, before the curtain rises, eavesdropping on the suppressed subtext, which is all about the large libidos of the fairies. Oberon and Titania and their court have come to seem dainty over the centuries, but (Carter is rudely and hilariously suggesting) they were monsters before the playwright got his hands on them (and theatrical tradition got its hands on *him*), and the woods they lived in were much more tangled. In this *Dream* there are no human characters: the whole range of *species* has been readjusted by the addition of a creature so satisfyingly exotic – a gilded hermaph-rodite, Carter's revision of the lovely Indian 'boy' ('Misinforma-tion. The patriarchal version' (*BV* 66)) Oberon and Titania squabble over in Shakespeare – that the fairies start to look ordinarily matter-of-fact, almost. So that, although she has shifted the whole action in the direction of fantasy, the effect is to *naturalize* us in this landscape – for the duration, while her story-teller's powers last. This is the real life of fantasy, she's saying. The lesser fairies all have colds in the head, and the wood, though pleasantly labyrinthine, is irretrievably *English*, not a patch on the forests of the Gothic north ... Shakespeare's text is reattached, via this umbilical cord of a narrative, to an imaginary matrix. Going 'behind' his text you free up the future, patch him into the quilt of writing once again. One should not overdo the domestic imagery, however. Home, in this symbolic economy, is just another topographical allegory, another stopping-off place on the picaresque trail. Carter's only novel of this decade, *Nights at the Circus*, published with a flourish by Carmen Callil at Chatto and Windus in 1984, chronicles a gargantuan series of adventures set at the turn of the last century, in the spacious realms of alterity. Since this is a book that is punctuated by somersaults of self-consciousness ('bums aloft' (NC 7)), I shall quote from one of the passages in which it turns round and looks at itself rather than producing my own paraphrase:

'A motley crew, indeed – a gaggle of strangers drawn from many diverse countries. Why, you might have said we constituted a microcosm of humanity, that we were an emblematic company, each signifying a different proposition in the great syllogism of life. The hazards of the journey reduced us to a little band of pilgrims abandoned in the wilderness upon whom the wilderness acted like a moral magnifying glass, exaggerating the blemishes of some and bringing out the finer points in those whom we thought had none. Those of us who learned the lessons of experience have ended their journeys already. Some who'll never learn are tumbling back to civilization as fast as they can as blissfully unenlightened as they ever were.' (NC 279)

This mock-instructive speech is given to wizened little Lizzie, the heroine's minder, another avatar of the author in granny/Mother Goose mode. (She's also a Sicilian witch, an anarchist plotter, a Bolshevik messenger linking literature-land and history.) One of the book's most striking effects – much rehearsed by Carter in the short stories – is the way the narrative labour is shared out, intercutting the third person with speeches, inset tales, metafictional overviews, and so forth. All of these voices are generously endowed with the kind of dubious plausibility that comes from the suspicion that they are making it up as they go along, *just like the author*, so that the reader is often treated to the uncanny feeling that he or she is being addressed from behind their masks by characters who know they are on stage. For instance, in the passage above it is the readers' journeys ('Some are tumbling back to civilization') that are being described, as well as the characters'. You are looking in a mirror.

The central thread, though – and the slowest and most overarching somersault – is provided by the narrative competition between our heroine Fevvers and journalist Walser: is this heavyweight Cockney trapeze artiste with wings a fraud, or a freak, or something else again? From the first moments of their opening interview, Californian Walser (a latter-day reincarnation of the Carter Jack-the-lad, the would-be giant killer, the realist, with 'a thatch of unruly flaxen hair, a ruddy, pleasant, square-jawed face and eyes the cool grey of scepticism' (NC 10)) finds himself caught up in an 'act' that will unravel his world-picture, and re-write his 'story' for him. When he runs away with the circus on its Imperial Russian tour, in the mask of a clown, he is hollowed out, inwardly scrambled, and patched back together again, remade by his experience in precisely the way the traditional picaresque hero never is. Whereas Fevvers, though she runs out of peroxide and breaks a wing, stays her own woman throughout, and keeps her mystery, the picaresque heroine whose experience rolls off her like water off a duck's back, or almost, even when she's enjoying her happy ending basking 'in the light of his grey eyes' (NC 293), which *now* reflect her with a lover's magical, transforming faith, despite (as it turns out) the fact that one of her mythic attributes – her virginity – was indeed a hoax.

So Fevvers is a fictive mutant, 'a new kind of being'. Except that, of course, iconographically speaking, she's far from original. She's Leda *and* the swan, she's the Winged Victory of Samothrace, she's an angel, even. The image of the woman with wings has served throughout the centuries as a carrier of men's meanings, and at the turn of the century in particular this time-honoured icon had a new lease of life. W.B. Yeats, for instance, circles round her in some of his most urgently visionary moments, not only in the poem, 'Leda and the Swan', but also in 'Sailing to Byzantium' and 'Byzantium', where a golden bird symbolizes 'the artifice of eternity'. These poems were written a bit late for the new century's dawn, but it was certainly Yeats's *fin de siècle* fascination with time's turning points, the magic intersections between history and myth (human and divine), which led him into such speculations. Marina Warner's description of the meanings of the

Nike (Winged Victory) in *Monuments and Maidens* helps explain the figure's power: 'The figure of Nike ... cancels time's inauspicious vigil on her subject's lives; she materialises as form in art the point at which the destiny of a single person converges auspiciously with time.... She has become conscious of our passage into the future.'[5] This sounds very grand, but as Warner also reminds us, Victory – like all traditional allegories – became pretty well anybody's property. In 1900 she was leading General Sherman's horse in New York; in 1911, she settled on the bonnet of Rolls-Royces in the form of the Silver Lady, and in the same year she turned up (gilded) on the Victoria monument in the Mall. She was already working as a logo, too, for Votes for Women, and as a cigar label.[6] In other words, Carter's creation of Fevvers as the heroine of the century's turn is an elaborate piece of revisionist mischief.

Fevvers is a symbol come to life *as a character*, who makes meanings on her own account, and evades the symbol-hunters who try to murder, vitrify, petrify, and pin her down. Early on she narrowly escapes becoming a May Day sacrifice for a Rosicrucian in search of immortal life, and later she very nearly becomes a Yeatsian golden bird (*à la Fabergé*) in St Petersburg. Again, Warner is a help; though she was not, of course, thinking about Carter's book, their coincidence is serendipitous. The point about nearly all of those larger-than-life female figures, she says, was that they had no character (she is using the Statue of Liberty to make her point):

> We can all take up occupation of Liberty, male, female, aged, children, she waits to enfold us in her meaning. But a male symbol like Uncle Sam relates to us in a different way.... The female form tends to be perceived as generic and universal.... We can all live inside Britannia or Liberty's skin, they stand for us regardless of sex, yet we cannot identify with them as characters. Uncle Sam and John Bull are popular figures, they can be grim, sly, feisty, pathetic, absurd, for they have personality. Liberty, like many abstract concepts expressed in the feminine, is in deadly earnest and one-dimensional.... *Liberty is not representing her own freedom.*[7]

Nor was Victory representing her own triumph. What Carter does is give Fevvers the mobility, particularity, weight, and humour of a character, and so give her back her gender. Fevvers uses signs as well as being one. Yeats in the Leda poem produces a grand rhetorical question: 'Did she put on his knowledge with his power...?' Well, annoyingly enough, yes, in this version. Fevvers' other name, we recall, is Sophia, which means wisdom. And she is certainly street-wise when it comes to thwarting the designs of magi and symbol-collectors and literary men. Even in the opening interview with Walser, she and Lizzie let the cat out of the bag several times, as (for instance) when she is musing on the decline of business in the motherly brothel where she was brought up:

> 'I put it down to the influence of *Baudelaire*, sir.'
> 'What's this?' cried Walser, amazed enough to drop his professional imperturbability.
> 'The French poet, sir; a poor fellow who loved whores not for the pleasure of it but, as he perceived it, the *horror* of it, as if we was, not working women doing it for money but *damned souls*.' (*NC* 38)

That 'sir' is a broad signal, a wink and a nudge. (Compare Lizzie, a bit later, on Shakespeare: 'We dearly love the Bard, sir' (*NC* 53)). Not only is Fevvers not a well-behaved modernist symbol; she is not a conventional 'character' either, but like Lizzie and the rest of the cast, plays author on occasion too.

Which brings me back to the narrative strategies of *Nights at the Circus*. Its plot takes us to the very edge of history, to peer over into a culture not yet colonized by our time-scheme, 'in that final little breathing-space before history *as such* extended its tentacles to grasp the entire globe' (*NC* 265). Now you see it, now you don't: there is no timelessness left, and that is at once a grievous loss, and a reminder (on this score the book is shamelessly didactic) that *everything* is in history now, the thing to do is to add in the outlaws and the ex-gods and the animals and the symbols and the freaks and the fools we edit out from the real, by which means we sustain an imaginary and lying kingdom of changelessness. Lizzie again: 'It's not the human "soul" that must be forged on the anvil of history but the anvil itself must be changed' (*NC* 240). This means that the novel aims not at an image of 'the artifice of eternity', but at discarding such mental refuges as it goes on, exploding them, leaving them behind. The 'O' of the circus ring is one such containing image; the clown troupe's dance of death is another; the Siberian prison built on the model of Bentham's panopticon is yet another. In the last analysis there are no alternative worlds, the 'other' is a myth, and the clowns, those 'whores of mirth' (*NC* 119) who are 'licensed to commit licence and yet forbidden to act' (*NC* 151), are a pun on chaos and stasis, the stuff of nightmare. The point of picaresque for Carter is that it moves inexorably onward, ever onward, generating stories out of stories. She wrote in 1985 that she liked 'to create complex, many-layered narratives that play tricks with time. And also, to explore ideas, although for me, that is the same thing as telling stories since, for me, a narrative is an argument stated in fictional terms' (*YS* 7). She was referring to writing for radio, but it is not at all a bad description of *Nights at the Circus*. It was a point of pride with her, by now, to insist that art was useful, and that the kind of fictional play she went in for might be satiric, utopian, dystopian, whatever, but *not* iconic or self-sealed. 'Fine art, that exists for itself alone, is art in a final state of impotence' (*SW* 13). Her narrative utopia – her idea of an idyll for the writer – is a dialogue with the reader, a sort of deconstructive communion, with the whole panorama and the enormous cast full of life and detail, and yet at the same time palpably unreal – merely a world populated by our changeful symbols, ourselves.

In the course of writing *Nights at the Circus* Angela Carter became pregnant – and her son, Alexander, was born in November 1983, months before it was published. She had used pregnancy as a plot device, a way of ending a novel, in *Heroes and Villains* (1969) first, in *New Eve* very elaborately indeed, so that it turns into an evolutionary rerun, with branches of the family tree for archaeopterix and other intermediate beings missed out first time round. She had trouble with endings once she had taken to using the picaresque format of allegorical travels, and wanted them to stay 'open'. And it wasn't too different with her life. She and Mark Pearce had 'settled down' over the years, but in a most vagrant fashion. She had travelled all over the place for jobs, residencies, and tours, and the Clapham house was always being changed around (her friend Christine moved on quite shortly), and was never finished. 'At home' they cooked, decorated, gardened, collected cats, kites, prints, paintings, gadgets, all piecemeal. The house became filled with the jetsam of their enthusiasms. Mark worked as a potter for a while, and made plates that were beautiful, but also enormous, so that they hardly fitted on the makeshift kitchen table, and you felt like a guest at a giants' feast. The two of them had taken to wearing identical surplus navy greatcoats outdoors, announcing their unanimity, and accentuating their height. Domestically they communed in silence, which was very much Mark's speciality, though she was pretty good at it too. They conspired to present their relationship as somehow *sui generis*, like a relation between creatures of different species who both happened to be tall – they had nothing much conventionally 'in common', of course, except that they were both eccentrics, stubborn, intransigent, wordlessly intimate. She did not, she said, study to conceive, simply found herself pregnant and decided to go ahead with it. An aged *primagravida*, she joked, but obviously her condition underlined the difference in their ages, and made her granny-disguise the more outrageous. In the November, in her last weeks, and on the day after judging the Booker (which went to J. M. Coetzee), she developed high blood pressure and was hospitalized. From hospital she wrote me a furious letter:

> my blood pressure rating has not been improved by my second run-in with the consultant obstetrician. Every time I remember what she said, I feel raptly incredulous and racked by impotent fury. Although at the time I said nothing because I could not believe my ears.
>
> So she says: 'How are you feeling?'
>
> 'Fine but apprehensive,' I say, 'not of the birth itself but of the next 20 years.'
>
> 'How is your husband feeling?' she asked.
>
> I paused to think of the right way of putting it and she said quickly: 'I know he's only your common-law husband.'
>
> While I was digesting this, she pressed down on my belly so I couldn't move and said:
>
> 'Of course you've done absolutely the right thing by *not* having an abortion but now is the time to contemplate adoption and I urge you to think about it very seriously.'
>
> That is *exactly* what she said! Each time I think about it, the adrenalin surges through my veins. I want to *kill* this woman. I want the B.M.A. to crucify her. I want to rip out her insides.
>
> Anyway, then she said: 'Its [sic] policy of the hospital to put older women into hospital for the last two weeks of pregnancy and I'll be generous, you can go home to collect your nightie & be back in an hour.'
>
> Nobody had told me about this policy before & I feel she may have made it up on the spur of the moment. Needless to say, she then buggered off back to her private practice. Was she being punitive? Why didn't I kick her in the crotch, you may ask. Why didn't I cry,

shreik [sic] & kick my heels on the ground, demanding she be forthwith stripped of her degrees & set to cleaning out the latrines. Why did I *come in*, after all that! Everybody else in this hospital is so nice & kind & sensible & sympathetic. There would have been a round of *applause* if I'd kicked her in the crotch. But, anyway, it turns out that I'm not in here for nothing – this ward is full of women with high blood pressure, swollen feet & the thing they make you collect your piss for, the dreaded protein in the urine. The doctor who looked at me today said they all spent a lot of time patching things up after my consultant, who is evidently famed for making strong women break down. Evidently I can agitate to go home again on Monday if my blood pressure has gone down.

'What about the consultant's weekly clinic?' I said, because I'm supposed to go to it.

'Dodge her,' the doctor said. The doctor is a slip of a right-on sister young enough to be my daughter. The consultant is a Thatcher-clone – evidently a Catholic, I'm told – old enough to be my mother. I am the uneasy filling in this sandwich.

A good example, this, of the way motherhood is used as a means of denying a woman's own meanings, taking away her choices, extruding her from normality's roster. Actually, the birth went all right, and, despite the seemingly inevitable hospital infection, Angela was able to rejoice from the beginning in Alex's Caravaggiesque beauty. But one can see how hard it was for her, at times, to make up her life as she went along. The writing in this letter belongs to a genre she disliked – the low mimetic, the language that reproduces the world. Small wonder she preferred surreal and metaleptic transformations, nothing to do with autobiography, or confession, or testament. But that seeming impersonality was, I'm arguing, entirely personal at base – a refusal to be placed or characterized or *saved* from oneself.

There are strange signs, as the millennium nears its end, that one of the most enduring, powerful, silly, and suggestive ways of thinking about artistic originality – one of the great myths about art – is at last becoming *scrutable*. I mean the notion that books are brain-children, and that therefore only male writers, in the last analysis, are haunted enough by the *metaphoric* mystery of creation to make work of real depth and intensity, make it new. Here is George Steiner, in *Real Presences*, with the big question: 'Is the biological capacity for procreation, for engendering formed life which is cardinal to woman ... so creative, so fulfilling, as to subvert, as to render comparatively pallid, the begetting of fictional personae which is the matter of drama and of so much representative art?'[8] Steiner says he does not know the answer, but obviously he thinks he does. What is interesting, actually, is that the issue surfaces in his consciousness in this form. I would say it was there for precisely the reason Angela pointed out in her piece on gender and writing ('Notes From the Front Line'): because women's fertility is *no longer involuntary*; you no longer have to choose between the (sexual) life and the work.

One small side-effect of this enormous cultural shift, which we have not at all yet come to terms with, is that the old metaphors about artistic parturition are being destablized. Christine Brooke-Rose, smarting from a whole professional lifetime's battle with the originality-police, sums up the mythology: 'Gender, genre, genius, genesis: all come from the same Indo-European root *gen*: to beget/ to be born. Only man begets, woman bears and travails: genius vs. work.'[9] That is, the men are associated with the dicey, ambivalent, inspirational one-off. In a way, as Brooke-Rose says, it is very close to the argument over ordaining women priests in the Church of England – 'the divine and metaphoric power of producing one thing out of another thing through the word'[10] is what is at stake. Not whether women have it, by the way – but (surely) that no one does. The real threat is to the Mystery itself. If you can no longer glorify the perverse, willed hubris of authorship by contrasting it with women's natural function, then a whole way of characterizing Art is slipping. Whoops.

One more piece of evidence for this *fin de siècle* phenomenon: in *Foucault's Pendulum* (1988) by Umberto Eco, it is the hero's girlfriend, the mother of his child, who demystifies the whole paranoid plot about unlimited semiosis, (male) overinterpretation. When Eco talked on the same topic at a Cambridge seminar (which also included Brooke-Rose), he revealed something of the underground connection he had spotted between the mystification of origins and originality, and the metaphoric substitutions for the life of the body: 'if a movement goes from A to B, then there is no force on earth that will be able to make it go from B to A.... Time is irreversible.' And for an example, he offers St Thomas Aquinas on virginity: 'Aquinas ... wonders whether a woman who has lost her virginity can be returned to her original undefiled condition.

Thomas's answer is clear, God may forgive her and ... may, by performing a miracle, give back her bodily integrity. But even God cannot cause what has been not to have been.'[11] Even Aquinas (even Aquinas's God) suspects that there's a limit to one's powers to make one's own meanings in *this* context. It's perhaps a far-fetched analogy, and yet, of course, the point is that the cardinal difference between men's and women's relations to their bodies, based on the equation of women = nature *is* ancient, embedded in our meanings. Women's bodies becoming part of culture is bound to be more disorienting than we can quickly recognize. Is Eco recreating the nature/culture binary divide? He seems to be arguing that the excesses of contemporary poststructuralist theory are the latest version of a Gnostic mystique of mind: 'The universe becomes one big hall of mirrors'; 'Gnosticism ... developed a rejection syndrome *vis-à-vis* both time and history.'[12] You can see how tricky this argument is: women writers and theorists have entered the hall of mirrors in droves this century, and have unwritten the histories. But the palace of unlimited semiosis turns out, for some at least – and among them I would include Carter – to be a bit like a mausoleum. Like Eco she wants to historicize, and secularize the Gnostic Demiurge.

It suits my purpose here to refer to cosmopolitan figures like Eco and Brooke-Rose, because otherwise I realize that I'm in danger of making Carter's focus on family trees and Englishness and Shakespeare, in her last novel *Wise Children* (1991), sound like a piece of Anglo-Saxon pragmatism, returning home at last, experimental wild oats sown. Not a bit of it. When she made parenthood her theme, it was parenthood literary, literal and lateral, with twins as mirrors to each other, illegitimate histories, left-handed genealogies, a whole carnival of the dispossessed. It is only that she understood the carnival pleasure of the text not as an ideal openness, but as having necessary limits:

> It's interesting that Bakhtin became very fashionable in the 1980s, during the demise of the particular kind of theory that would have put all kinds of questions around the whole idea of the carnivalesque. I'm thinking about Marcuse and repressive desublimation, which tells you exactly what carnivals are for. The carnival has to stop. The whole point of the feast of fools is that things went on as they did before, after it stopped. (*NW* 188)

This was the point she had made about the hopelessness of

circularity and the clowns in *Nights at the Circus*, and the climactic scene – or rather one of the climactic scenes – in *Wise Children* (nothing comes singly in this book) represents an optimistic replay of this same encounter with the limit. The narrator Dora in her ribald old age finally falls into bed with her beloved uncle and surrogate father Peregrine, a Falstaffian figure who is even older, and the shattering event is recorded from the point of view of her twin, Nora, since for the moment our tale-teller was otherwise engaged:

> There was just one ecstatic moment, she opined, when she thought the grand bouncing on the bed upstairs – remember Perry was a *big* man – would bring down that chandelier and all its candles, smash, bang, clatter, and the swagged ceiling, too; bring the house down, fuck the house down, come ('cum?') all over the posh frocks and the monkey jackets and the poisoned cake and the lovers, mothers, sisters, shatter the lenses that turned our lives into peepshows, scatter little candleflames like an epiphany on every head, cover over all the family, the friends, the camera crews, with plaster dust and come and fire.
>
> But such was not to be. There are limits to the power of laughter and though I may hint at them from time to time, I do not propose to step over them. (*WC* 220)

If carnival represents the promiscuous and horizontal axis of narrative relations, then at carnival's end we return to verticality – the line, the family, history's determinings, time's irreversibility. When present-day Dora contemplates her youthful self in the 1930s film of *A Midsummer Night's Dream* she finally sees the point of the awful kitsch literalness of the film's illusion (as opposed to her beloved theatre): 'I understood the thing I'd never grasped back in those days, when I was young, before I lived in history. When I was young, I'd wanted to be ephemeral ... to live in just the glorious moment, the rush of blood, the applause.... Tomorrow never comes. But, oh yes, tomorrow *does* come alright.... But if you've put your past on celluloid, it lasts' (*NC* 125). Compare *The Passion of New Eve* on Hollywood symbols – 'A critique of these symbols is a critique of our lives' (*PNE* 6) – the more so when you take into account their complicity with cash and power.

*Wise Children* traces the history of the Hazard theatrical dynasty, from its nineteenth-century heyday, when its members colonized their world (or at least the colonies) bearing Shakespeare to the sticks, through to the twentieth-century upturning of that imperial theme, which finds the bard's plays being travestied in other media, and the stage itself upstaged by television. In the process, a certain democratization has set in. The bastard (and childless) branch of the family, Dora and Nora, who belonged to show biz and vaudeville, find that over their long lifetimes the father who disowned them has (largely unknowingly) joined the ranks of the unrespectable, while people are doing PhDs on that kitsch movie. In their youth Dora and Nora swap sexual partners and play each others' roles like boys playing girls in the Forest of Arden; in the 1930s their father plays Shakespeare himself in a cool musical (*What! You Will!*) with parts for his bastard daughters. The book is littered with allusions that disseminate Shakespeare, spread him around, reinvent him as latterday demotic. Or perhaps only restore him to his pre-canonized self. 'Shakespeare just isn't an intellectual' Carter announced in a 1991 interview:

> intellectuals ... are still reluctant to treat him as popular culture.... You mention folk culture and people immediately assume you're going to talk about porridge and clog dancing, there's this William Morris and Arnold Wesker prospect, truly the bourne from which no traveller returns. Shakespeare, like Picasso, is one of the great hinge-figures that sum up the past – one of the great Janus-figures that sum up the past as well as opening all the doors towards the future ... I like *A Midsummer Night's Dream* almost beyond reason, because it's beautiful and funny and camp – and glamorous, and cynical.... English popular culture is very odd, it's got some very odd and unreconstructed elements in it. There's no other country in the world where you have pantomime with men dressed as women and women dressed as men.... It's part of the great tradition of British art, is all that 'smut' and transvestism and so on. (*NW* 186–7)

In the Preface to her 1990 fairy-tale anthology she had speculated that perhaps today's equivalent to the old oral tradition was to be found in the soap opera and the dirty joke – genres *Wise Children* also celebrates. *Performance* is a great leveller and so is audience participation. Dora, performer turned narrator, got a crash course in literature while she played the role of Muse to a writer who condescended to drink himself to death in Hollywood – 'I was busy with my studies (W. for Wedekind)' (*WC* 144). Carter's narrator and her twin share the performer's ability to distinguish between their parts and their possible selves – a consciousness heightened by their mirror-imaging of each other. It is no accident Dora mentions Wedekind, for Carter had Wedekind's Lulu very much in mind in *Wise Children*, and she gives her twins the looks of Louise Brooks, who played Lulu in Pabst's film. They share, too, what Carter called the rare 'negative virtue' demonstrated by Lulu/Louise, 'her lack of hypocrisy' (*NS* 121), though they are a comic variant on the theme, *femmes fatales* who merely doubled for the part, laughed, and grew old.

'All fiction', she agreed with Balzac, 'is symbolic autobiography.'[13] In *Wise Children* 75-year-old Nora and Dora are presented with the babies they never had, and luckily – they failed this time, unusually for Carter characters, to burn the house down – they have a home to go to. Granny's of course. In this novel the ritual deconstruction is reserved, not for the house, but for the figure of the patriarch:

> 'And tonight he had an imitation look, even when he was crying, especially when he was crying, like one of those great, big, papier-mâché heads they have in the Notting Hill parade....'
> Nora sunk in thought for a hundred yards.
> 'D'you know, I sometimes wonder if we haven't been making him up all along,' she said. 'If he isn't just a collection of our hopes and dreams and wishful thinking in the afternoons. Something to set our lives by, like the old clock in the hall, which is real enough, in itself, but which we've got to wind up to make it go.'
> 'Oh, very profound, very deep.' (*WC* 230)

This sense of the way in which the objects of desire and fear can change and fade is one of the secrets of her style's exhilarations. Vertigo, the loss of stability, is meat and drink to Carter. A final quotation from a letter of 1989 shows the process at work in a different context. She and Mark and Alex had taken to exploring London by water, on a canal boat:

> the canals are wonderful.... You get this Ophelia-style view of the canal bank, huge juicy plants & flowers & grasses; and we saw herons, & a king-fisher, & it was that frail, chilly, early spring that is so English, & the East End – we went through Hackney – is now really one vast nature reserve, mile after mile of abandoned factories returning to the wild. I kept thinking: 'This dereliction produced the wealth that made London the richest city in the world.' All gone. It was like Ozymandias.

She gets from Ophelia to Shelley's tyrant in one pastoral swoop. 'All gone' is a sign of liberation – Time will fix tyrants, too, if someone remembers to wind up the clock.

The 'post'-ness of Carter's world-picture (post-industrial, post-imperial) suggests an obvious label: postmodern. I have been reluctant to use it, however, because it seems to me to convey a kind of terminal reflexiveness, a notion of fiction as a vacated funhouse, a spatialized model for narrative, which I don't think fits exactly. She had a position on the politics of textuality. She went in for the proliferation, rather than the death, of the author. Labels like Linda Hutcheon's 'historiographic metafiction', or Brooke-Rose's 'palimpsest history', come closer to the mark, since they put the time dimension back in. Then there is still the feminist to characterize. In *New Eve* and *Wise Children*, in particular, Carter speaks the same language as someone like Hélène Cixous.

> The origin is a masculine myth.... The question 'Where do children come from?' is basically a masculine, much more than a feminine, question. The quest for origins, illustrated by Oedipus, doesn't haunt a feminine unconscious. Rather it's the beginning, or beginnings ... starting on all sides at once, that makes a feminine writing.... When a woman writes in nonrepression she passes on her others, her abundance of non-ego/s in a way that destroys the form of the family structure.... She writes of not-writing, non-happening.[14]

And this is the point where Carter parted company with Cixous and 'écriture féminine'. She admired 'utopian anti-art', but 'the problem with literature is that it's impure' (*NW* 192) – a problem she addressed through the use of pastiche, parody, quotation marks, representations. ... As it turned out, she was by temperament and by self-invention a tale-spinner, interested not in 'not-writing', but in conjuring up the power of voices in the dark.

Angela Carter discovered she had lung cancer in the early spring of 1991, and died less than a year later. She had given up smoking years before, when she was pregnant with Alex, but, as one medic said to her she had not given up living and walking in London. She died at home in her own bed, having set her affairs in order, at a moment – it now seems in retrospect – when her genius was about to be universally acknowledged, and her work recognized for its savage intelligence, its rich humour, and its bold inventiveness. But this is probably an illusion created by the change in tone enjoined on us all by the fact of her premature death. If she'd stayed around, her canonization would almost certainly have been postponed. Now that her voice has been silenced, we're left with the orphaned words on the page, which line up and behave.

One of the last things she wrote, *The Holy Family Album* (1991) for television, got her into trouble of a characteristic kind. It attacked God the Father for the tortures inflicted on His son in the name of Love, but in the cause of Power, a piece of deliberate blasphemy against the Almighty Author. And a plea for mortality. *Flesh comes to us out of history.* Nothing stays, endings are final, which is why they are also beginnings.

# Notes

## PROLOGUE

1. Margaret Atwood's obituary appeared in the London *Observer* for 23 Feb. 1992, Carmen Callil's in the *Sunday Times* on the same day.
2. Roland Barthes, 'The Death of the Author' (1968), in *Image–Music–Text*, essays selected and translated by Stephen Heath (London: Fontana/Collins, 1977), 142–8, at p.142.
3. ibid. 146.

## CHAPTER 1. BEGINNING

1. Angela Carter, 'The Curious Room', *American Ghosts & Old World Wonders* (London: Vintage, 1994), 121–39, at p. 127.
2. Rosalind Coward, *Our Treacherous Hearts: Why Women Let Men Get their Way* (London: Faber and Faber, 1992), 91–2.
3. Susan Sontag, 'Notes on Camp' (1964), in *A Susan Sontag Reader* (New York: Vintage Books, 1983), 105–19, at p. 118.
4. ibid. 114, 109.
5. ibid. 113.
6. ibid. 116–17.
7. Gerardine Meaney, *(Un)like Subjects: Women, Theory, Fiction* (London: Routledge, 1993), 91.
8. Marc O'Day, 'Mutability is having a Field day: The Sixties Aura of Carter's Bristol Trilogy', in Lorna Sage (ed.), *Flesh and the Mirror* (London: Virago, 1994).

## CHAPTER 2. MIDDLE

1. Angela Carter, 'A Souvenir of Japan', *Fireworks* (1974; London: Virago, 1988), 1–11, at p. 9.

2. Hazel Rowley, *Christina Stead* (Heinemann Australia, 1993), 10.
3. Roland Barthes, *Empire of Signs* (1970); trans. Richard Howard (London: Jonathan Cape, 1983), 62.
4. ibid. 9.
5. ibid. 10.
6. Norman Mailer, *The Prisoner of Sex* (New York, 1971), 142.
7. Barthes, *Empire of Signs*, 4.
8. Jorge Luis Borges, *The Book of Imaginary Beings*, trans. Norman Thomas di Giovanni (1969: Harmondsworth: Penguin, 1974), 67-8.
9. Simone de Beauvoir, *All Said and Done* (1972), trans. P. O'Brian (Harmondsworth: Penguin, 1977), 491.
10. Stephen Jay Gould, *Wonderful Life: The Burgess Shale and the Nature of History* (1989; London: Hutchinson Radius, 1990), 48, 96.
11. ibid. 309, 319.
12. Jack Zipes, *Breaking the Magic Spell: Radical Theories of Folk and Fairy Tales* (London: Heinemann, 1979), 18–19.
13. Ernst Bloch, *The Principle of Hope* (1971), quoted in Zipes, *Breaking the Magic Spell*, 129.

## CHAPTER 3. ENDING

1. Angela Carter, 'Notes from the Front Line', in Michelene Wandor (ed.), *On Gender and Writing* (London: Pandora Press, 1983), 69-77, at p. 73.
2. Christina Stead (1968); repr. in *Ocean of Story* (Harmondsworth: Viking Penguin, 1985), 3.
3. Christina Stead, *The Saltzburg Tales* (1934; London: Virago, 1986), 38, 176–7.
4. Angela Carter, Introduction to C. Stead, *The Puzzleheaded Girl* (London: Virago, 1984), p. xiv.
5. Marina Warner, *Monuments and Maidens* (1985; London: Picador, 1987), 134–5.
6. ibid. 142–3.
7. ibid. 12 (emphasis added).
8. George Steiner, *Real Presences* (London: Faber & Faber, 1989), 207.
9. Christine Brooke-Rose, 'Illiterations', in *Stories, Theories and Things* (Cambridge: Cambridge University Press, 1991), 250–64 at p. 255.
10. ibid. 258.
11. Umberto Eco, *Interpretation and Overinterpretation*, with R. Rorty, J. Culler, and C. Brooke-Rose, ed. Stefan Collini (Cambridge: Cambridge University Press, 1992), 27–8.
12. ibid. 31, 35.
13. Angela Carter, Introduction to Walter de la Mare, *Memoirs of a*

*Midget* (Oxford: Oxford University Press, 1982), p. xxiii.
14. Hélène Cixous, 'La Sexe ou la tête?', *Les Cahiers du GRIF*, 13 (1976), 54–5; trans. A. Kuhn, 'Castration or Decapitation?' *Signs*, 7 (1981), 41–55.

# Select Bibliography

## WORKS BY ANGELA CARTER

### Novels

*Shadow Dance* (London: Heinemann, 1966) repr. as *Honeybuzzard* (New York: Simon & Schuster, 1966; London: Pan, 1968).

*The Magic Toyshop* (London: Heinemann, 1967; New York: Simon & Schuster, 1968; London: Virago, 1981; London: Vintage, 2006).

*Several Perceptions* (London: Heinemann, 1968; New York: Simon & Schuster, 1968; London: Pan, 1970).

*Heroes and Villains*, (London: Heinemann, 1969; New York: Simon & Schuster, 1969; Harmondsworth: Penguin, 1981).

*Love*, (London: Rupert Hart-Davis, 1971; rev. edn., London: Chatto & Windus, 1987; New York: Viking Penguin 1988; London: Picador, 1988).

*The Infernal Desire Machines of Doctor Hoffman* (London: Rupert Hart-Davis, 1972) repr. as *The War of Dreams* (New York: Bard/Avon Books, 1977; Harmondsworth: Penguin, 1982).

*The Passion of New Eve* (London: Gollancz, 1977; New York: Harcourt Brace Jovanovich, 1977; London: Virago, 1982).

*Nights at the Circus* (London: Chatto & Windus, 1984; New York: Viking, 1985; London: Pan, 1985).

*Wise Children* (London: Chatto & Windus, 1991; New York: Farrar, Straus, and Girous, 1992; London: Vintage, 1992; London: Vintage, 2006).

### Short stories

*Fireworks: Nine Profane Pieces* (London: Quartet Books, 1974; New York: Harper & Row, 1981; rev. edn. London: Chatto & Windus, 1987; London: Virago, 1988).

*The Bloody Chamber and Other Stories* (London: Gollancz, 1979; New York: Harper & Row, 1980; Harmondsworth: Penguin, 1981; London: Vintage, 2006).

*Black Venus's Tale*, with woodcuts by Philip Sutton (London: Next Editions in association with Faber, 1980).

*Black Venus* (London: Chatto & Windus, 1985) repr. as *Saints and Strangers*, (London: Pan, 1986; New York: Viking Penguin, 1987).

*American Ghosts & Old-World Wonders* (London: Chatto & Windus, 1993; London: Vintage, 1994).

*Burning your Boats: Collected Short Stories*, (London: Chatto & Windus, 1995; repr. London: Vintage, 1996).

## Children's Stories

*Miss Z. The Dark Young Lady*, illustrated by Keith Eros (London: Heinemann, 1970; New York: Simon & Schuster, 1970).

*The Donkey Prince*, illustrated by Keith Eros (New York: Simon & Schuster, 1970).

*Martin Leman's Comic and Curious Cats*, text by Angela Carter, illustrations by Martin Leman (London: Gollancz, 1979; London: Gollancz paperback, 1988).

*Moonshadow*, text by Angela Carter, idea and paintings by Justin Todd (London: Gollancz, 1982).

*Sea-Cat and Dragon-King*, (London: Bloomsbury, 2000).

## Verse

*Unicorn* (Leeds: Location Press, 1966).

## Radio Plays

*Come Unto These Yellow Sands: Four Radio Plays* (Newcastle upon Tyne: Bloodaxe Books, 1985; Dufour Editions, 1985; Newcastle upon Tyne: Bloodaxe paperback, 1985).

## Film and Television

Jordan, Neil (dir.), *The Company of Wolves* (ITC Entertainment/Palace Production 1984).

Wheatley, David (dir.), *The Magic Toyshop* (Granada TV, 1987).

'The Kitchen Child', *Short and Curlies* (Channel Four, 30 June 1990).

*The Holy Family Album* (Channel Four, 3 Dec. 1991).

## Non-Fiction

*The Sadeian Woman: An Exercise in Cultural History* (London: Virago, 1979) repr. a *The Sadeian Woman and the Ideology of Pornography* (New York: Pantheon, 1979).

Translator and Foreword, *The Fairy Tales of Charles Perrault*, (London: Gollancz, 1977; New York: Bard Books, 1979).

*Nothing Sacred: Selected Writings* (London: Virago, 1982, rev. edn., London; Virago, 1992).

Editor and translator, *Sleeping Beauty and Other Favourite Fairy Tales* (London: Gollancz, 1982; New York: Schoken, 1989; London: Gollancz paperback, 1991).

Introduction to Walter de La Mare, *Memoirs of a Midget* (Oxford: Oxford University Press, 1982).

Introduction to Christina Stead, *The Puzzleheaded Girl* (London: Virago, 1984).

Editor, *Wayward Girls and Wicked Women* (London: Virago, 1986).

Introduction to Gilbert Hernandez, *Duck Feet* (London: Titan Books, 1988).

*Images of Frida Kahlo* (London: Redstone Press, 1989).

Editor, *The Virago Book of Fairy Tales* (London: Virago, 1990; repr. as *Old Wives' Fairy Tale Book*, New York: David McKay, 1987; London: Virago, 1991).

Introduction to Charlotte Brontë, *Jane Eyre* (London: Virago, 1990).

*Expletives Deleted: Selected Writings* (London: Chatto & Windus, 1992; London: Vintage, 1993).

Editor, *The Second Virago Book of Fairy Tales* (London: Virago, 1992; London: Virago, 1993).

*The Curious Room: Collected Dramatic Works* (London: Chatto & Windus, 1996).

*Shaking a Leg: Collected Journalism and Writings* (London: Chatto & Windus, 1997).

## Uncollected Material

'Fred Jordan, Singer,' *New Society*, 23 Feb. 1967, 283.

'The Good Old Songs', *New Society*, 21 Mar. 1968, 422–3.

'Stealing is Bad Karma', *Listener*, 83, 25 June 1970, 855.

'Living in London – X', *London Magazine*, 10 Mar. 1971, 49–56.

'Pupils' Voices', *New Society*, 15 June 1972, 559–60.

'Donovan's Dog,' *Nova*, Oct. 1973, 38–9, 41.

'The Hidden Child', *New Society*, 6 Mar. 1975, 595–6.

'Wolfe at the Writer's Door,' *New Society*, 23 Oct. 1975, 220–1.

'Giant's Playtime', *New Society*, 29 Jan. 1976, 227–8.

'The Power of Porn', *Observer*, 10 Apr. 1977, 9.

'Family Life – 6, Time to Tell the Time', *New Review*, 4/42, Sept. 1977, 41–6.

'Weaver of Dreams from the Stuff of Nightmares', *Guardian*, 26 Oct. 1979, 11.

'Bored, Bothered and Bewildered', *Times Educational Supplement*, 7 Dec. 1979, 4.

'Much, Much Stranger than Fiction', *New Society*, 20–27 Dec. 1979, ix–xi.

'The Language of Sisterhood', in Leonard Michaels and Christopher Ricks (eds.) *The State of the Language* (Berkeley, Calif: University of California Press, 1980), 226–34.

'Yen in South Ken', *New Society*, 20 Mar. 1980, 608–9.

'The Apotheosis of John Doe: Being There,' *New Society*, 21 Aug. 1980, 368–9.

'Being Oneself at School,' *New Society*, 11 June 1981, 443–4.

'Through the Tudor Keyhole: *Artists of the Tudor Court*' (exhibition), *New Society*, 21 July 1983, 98–9.

'Occidentalism,' *Guardian*, 3 Apr. 1986.

'Truly, It Felt Like Year One', in Sara Maitland (ed.), *Very Heaven: Looking Back at the 1960s* (London: Virago, 1988), 209–16.

## WORKS ON ANGELA CARTER

### Monographs

Crofts, Charlotte, *'Anagrams of Desire': Angela Carter's Writing for Radio, Film and Television* (Manchester: Manchester University Press, 2003).

Day, Aidan, *Angela Carter: The Rational Glass* (Manchester: Manchester University Press, 1998).

Gamble, Sarah, *Angela Carter: Writing from the Front Line* (Edinburgh: Edinburgh University Press, 1997).

Gamble, Sarah, *Angela Carter: A Literary Life* (Basingstoke/New York: Palgrave Macmillan, 2006.)

Lee, Alison, *Angela Carter* (New York: Twayne Publishers, 1997).

Peach, Linden, *Angela Carter* (Basingstoke: Macmillan, 1998).

Tucker, Lindsay, *Critical Essays on Angela Carter* (New York: Prentice International, 1998).

### Interviews, Profiles and Obituaries

Stott, Catherine, 'Runaway to the Land of Promise', *Guardian*, 10 Aug. 1972, 9.

Bedford, Les, 'Angela Carter: An Interview', Sheffield University Television, February, 1977.

Sage, Lorna, 'The Savage Sideshow', *New Review*, 4/39–40, July 1977, 51–7.

Watts, Janet, 'Sade and the Sexual Struggle', *Observer Magazine*, 25 Mar. 1979, 54–5.

Hamilton, Alex, 'Sade and Prejudice', *Guardian*, 30 Mar. 1979, 15.

Mortimer, John, 'The Stylish Prime of Miss Carter', *Sunday Times*, 24 Jan. 1982, 36.

McEwan, Ian, 'Sweet Smell of Excess', *Sunday Times Magazine*, 9 Sept. 1984, 42–4.

Haron, Mary, 'I'm a Socialist, Damn it! How can you expect me to be interested in fairies?', *Guardian*, 25 Sept. 1984, 10.

Haffenden, John, 'Magical Mannerist', *Literary Review*, Nov. 1984, 34–8. *Book Four*, Channel Four, 2 Dec. 1984. Repr. in Haffenden, John, (ed.), *Novelists in Interview* (London: Methuen, 1985), 76–96.

Moi, Toril, 'Pornografi og Fantasi: om Kvinner, Klaer of Filosofi', *Vinduet*, 1/38, 1984, 17–21.

Goldsworthy, Kerryn, 'Angela Carter,' *Meanjin*, 44/1 (Adelaide, Mar. 1985), 4–13.

Cagney Watts, Helen, 'An Interview with Angela Carter', *Bête Noire*, 8 Aug. 1985, 161–76.

Smith, Anne, 'Myths and the Erotic', *Women's Review*, 1 Nov. 1985, 28–9.

Gristwood, Sarah, 'Not a Bad Lot,' *Guardian*, 29 Oct. 1986.

Waterson, Moira, 'Flights of Fancy in Balham', *Observer Magazine*, 9 Nov. 1986, 42–5.

Appignanesi, Lisa, *Angela Carter in Conversation*, London: ICA Video, 1987.

*Women Writers*, Channel Four, 26 Oct. 1987.

Mars-Jones, Adam, *Angela Carter in Conversation*, London: ICA Video.

Snitow, Ann, 'Conversation with a Necromancer', *Village Voice Literary Supplement*, 75, June 1989, 14–16.

Morgan-Griffiths, Laura, 'Well Wicked Times by Word of Mouth', *Observer*, 21 Oct. 1990, 5.

Clapp, Susannah, 'On Madness, Men and Fairy-Tales', *Independent on Sunday*, 9 June 1991, 26–7.

Kemp, Peter, 'Magical History Tour', *Sunday Times*, 9 June 1991, 6–7.

Sage, Lorna, 'Angela Carter Interviewed by Lorna Sage', in Malcolm Bradbury and Judith Cooke (eds.), *New Writing*, London: Minerva Press, 1992, 185–93.

*Times*, 'Angela Carter', 17 Feb. 1992, 15.

Sage, Lorna, 'The Soaring Imagination', *Guardian*, 17 Feb. 1992, 37.

*The Late Show*, BBC2, 18 Feb. 1992.

Coover, Robert, 'A Passionate Remembrance', *Guardian*, 18 Feb. 1992. Repr. in *The Review of Contemporary Fiction*, 14:3, fall 1994, 9–10.

Warner, Marina, 'Obituary: Angela Carter', *Independent*, 18 Feb. 1992.

Webb, W. L. 'Angela Carter, Rich in Rude Grace', *Guardian*, 20 Feb. 1992.

Atwood, Margaret, 'Magic Token Through the Dark Forest', *Observer*, (23 Feb. 1992, 61.

Callil, Carmen, 'Flying Jewellry', *Sunday Times*, 23 Feb. 1992, 6.

Rushdie, Salman, 'Angela Carter 1940–92: A Very Good Wizard, A Very

Dear Friend', *New York Times Book Review*, 8 Mar. 1992, 5.

Grove, Valerie, 'If I Should Die, Think Only This Of Me', *Times*, 27 Mar. 1992.

Sage, Lorna, 'Death of the Author', *Granta: Biography*, 41, autumn 1992, 233–54.

Evans, Kim (producer), 'Angela Carter's Curious Room', London: BBC1 Omnibus Video, 15 Sept. 1992.

Bradfield, Scott, 'Remembering Angela Carter', *Review of Contemporary Fiction*, 14:3, fall 1994, 90–3.

Katsavos, Anna, 'An Interview with Angela Carter', *Review of Contemporary Fiction*, 14:3, fall 1994, 11–17.

Barker, Paul, 'The Return of the Magic Story-Teller', *Independent on Sunday*, 8 Jan. 1995, 14–16.

Gerrard, Nicci, 'Angela Carter is Now More Popular Than Virginia Woolf', *Observer Life*, 9 July 1995, 20, 22–3.

## Collected Criticism

Sage, Lorna, (ed.), *Flesh and the Mirror: Essays on the Art of Angela Carter* (London: Virago Press, 1994).

Bristow, Joseph and Broughton, Trev Lynn, (eds.), *The Infernal Desires of Angela Carter: Fiction, Femininity, Feminism,* (Harlow: Addison Wesley Longman, 1997).

Easton, Alison, (ed.), *Angela Carter: Contemporary Critical Essays* (Basingstoke: Macmillan, 2000).

Roemer, Danielle M. and Bacchilegga, Cristina, (eds.), *Angela Carter and the Fairy Tale* (Detroit, MI: Wayne State University Press, 2001).

Pitchford, Nicola, *Tactical Readings: Feminist Postmodernism in the Novels of Kathy Acker and Angela Carter*, (London: Associated University Presses, 2002).

## Further Criticism

Alexander, Flora, *Contemporary Women Novelists* (London: Edward Arnold, 1989), 63–75.

Alvarez, Antonia, 'On Translating Metaphor', *Meta*, 38/2 (Sept. 1993), 479–90.

Anwell, Maggie, 'Lolita Meets the Werewolf: The Company of Wolves, in Lorraine Gamman and Margaret Marshment (eds.), *The Female Gaze: Women as Viewers of Popular Culture* (London: The Women's Press, 1988), 76–85.

Armitt, Lucie, *Theorising the Fantastic* (London: Arnold, 1996).

Armitt, Lucie, *Contemporary Women's Fiction and the Fantastic* (Basingstoke: Macmillan, 2000).

Bell, Michael, 'Narrations as Action: Goethe's "Bekenntnisse Einer Schönen Seele" and Angela Carter's *Nights at the Circus', German Life and Letters*, 45/1 (Jan. 1992), 16–32.

Blain, Virginia, *et al.* (eds.), *The Feminist Companion to Literature in English* (London: Batsford, 1990).

Bryant, Sylvia, 'Re-Constructing Oedipus through "Beauty and the Beast"', *Criticism*, 31/4, (fall 1984), 439–53.

Clark, Robert, 'Angela Carter's Desire Machine', *Women's Studies*, 14/2 (1987), 147–61.

Collick, John, 'Wolves through the Window: Writing Dreams/Dreaming Films/Filming Dreams', *Critical Survey*, 3/3 (1991), 283–9.

Cranny-Francis, Anne, *Feminist Fiction: Feminist Uses of Generic Fiction* (Cambridge: Polity Press, 1990).

Cronan, Rose Ellen, 'Through the Looking Glass: When Women Tell Fairy Tales,' in E. Abel *et al.* (eds.), *The Voyage In: Fictions of Female Development* (London: University Press of New England, 1983), 209–27.

Duncker, Patricia, 'Re-Imagining the Fairy Tales: Angela Carter's Bloody Chambers', *Literature and History*, 10/1 (spring 1984), 3–14.

Forsyth, Neil, 'A Letter from Angela Carter', in *The European English Messenger*, 4,1 (spring 1996), 11–13.

Fowl, Melinda G., 'Angela Carter's *The Bloody Chamber* Revisited', *Critical Survey*, 3/1 (1991), 67–79.

Gamble, Sarah, (ed.), *The Fiction of Angela Carter: A reader's guide to the essential criticism*, (Cambridge: Icon Books, 2001).

Gasiorek, Andrzej, *Post-War British Fiction: Realism and After* (London: Edward Arnold, 1995).

Gorra, Michael, 'Fiction Chronicle', *Hudson Review*, 40/1 (spring 1987), 136–48.

Hanson, Claire, 'Each Other: Images of Otherness in the Short Fiction of Doris Lessing, Jean Rhys and Angela Carter', *Journal of the Short Story in English*, 10 (spring 1988), 67–82.

Harman, Claire, 'Demon-Lovers and Sticking-plaster,' *Independent on Sunday* (30 October 1994), 37.

Joannou, Maroula, *Contemporary Women's Writing: From The Golden Notebook to The Colour Purple*, (Manchester: Manchester University Press, 2000).

Jordan, Elaine, 'Enthrallment: Angela Carter's Speculative Fictions', in Linda Anderson (ed.) *Plotting Change: Contemporary Women's Fiction* (London: Edward Arnold, 1990), 18–40.

Jordan, Elaine, 'The Dangers of Angela Carter' in Isobel Armstrong (ed.), *New Feminist Discourses* (London: Routledge, 1992), 119–31.

Jordan, Elaine, 'Down the Road, or History Rehearsed', in Francis Barker *et al.* (eds.), *Postmodernism and the Re-reading of Modernity* (Manchester: Manchester University Press, 1992), 159–79.

Kappeler, Susanne, *The Pornography of Representation* (Cambridge: Polity

Press, 1986).

Kenyon, Olga, *Writing Women*, (London: Pluto Press, 1991).

Llewellyn, Avis, 'Wayward Girls but Wicked Women?', in Gary Day and Clive Bloom (eds.), *Perspectives on Pornography* (London: Macmillan, 1988), 144–57.

Lokke, Kari E., '*Bluebeard* and *The Bloody Chamber*: The Grotesque of Self-Parody and Self-Assertion', *Frontiers*, 10/1 (1988), 7–12.

Makinen, Merja, 'Angela Carter's *The Bloody Chamber* and the Decolonization of Feminine Sexuality', *Feminist Review*, 42 (autumn, 1992), 2–15.

Matus, Jill, 'Blonde, Black and Hottentot Venus: Context and Critique in Angela Carter's "Black Venus"' *Studies in Short Fiction*, 28 (fall 1991), 467–76.

Meaney, Gerardine, *(Un)like Subjects: Women, Theory and Fiction* (London: Routledge, 1993).

Mills, Sara, Pearce, Lynne, *et al.*, *Feminist Readings/Feminists Reading* (Hemel Hempstead: Harvester, 1989).

Neumeier, Beate, 'Postmodern Gothic: Desire and Reality in Angela Carter's Writing', in Victor Sage and Allan Lloyd Smith, (eds.), *Modern Gothic: A Reader* (Manchester: Manchester University Press, 1996), 141–151.

Palmer, Pauline, 'From "Coded Mannequin" to Bird Woman: Angela Carter's Magic Flight' in Sue Roe (ed.) *Women Reading Women's Writing* (Brighton: Harvester, 1987), 177–205.

Parker, Emma, 'The Consumption of Angela Carter: Women, Food and Power' *Ariel: A Review of International English Literature*, 31:3 (July 2000), 141–69.

Punter, David, *The Literature of Terror: A History of Gothic Fictions from 1765 to the Present Day* (London: Longman, 1980), 396–400.

Punter, David, 'Angela Carter: Supersessions of the Masculine', *Critique: Studies in Modern Fiction*, 25/41 (summer 1984), 209–22, repr. in *The Hidden Script: Writing and the Unconscious* (London: Routledge, 1985), 28–42.

Rosinsky, Natalie M., *Feminist Futures: Contemporary Women's Speculative Fiction* (Michigan: UMI Research, 1982), 10–19.

Rubenstein, Roberta, 'Intersexions: Gender Metamorphosis in Angela Carter's *The Passion of New Eve* and Lois Gold's *A Sea-Change*', *Tulsa Studies in Women's Literature*, 12:1 (1993), 103–8.

Russo, Mary, *The Female Grotesque: Risk, Excess, and Modernity* (London: Routledge, 1995).

Sage, Lorna, 'Angela Carter', *Dictionary of Literary Biography, xiv. British Novelists since 1960*, ed. Jay L. Halio, (Detroit: Bruccoli Clark, 1983), Vol 1, 205–12.

Sage, Lorna, *Contemporary Writers: Angela Carter* (London: British Council leaflet, 1990).

Sage, Lorna, *Women in the House of Fiction* (Basingstoke: Macmillan, 1992), 168–77.

———, (ed.), *Flesh and the Mirror: Essays on the Art of Angela Carter* (London: Virago, 1994).

Sceats, Sarah, *Consumption and the Body in Contemporary Women's Fiction*, (London: Cambridge University Press, 2000).

See, Carolyn, 'Come On and See the Winged Lady', *New York Times*, 24 February 1985.

Smith, Ali, 'Get Carter', in Andrew Motion, (ed.), *Interrupted Lives*, (London: National Portrait Gallery Publications, 2004), 80–95.

Smith, Curtis C. (ed.), *Twentieth Century Science Fiction Writers* (Basingstoke: Macmillan, 1981).

Smith, Patricia Juliana, 'All You Need is Love: Angela Carter's Novel of Sixties Sex and Sensibility', *Review of Contemporary Fiction* (fall, 1994), 24–9.

Vallorani, Nicoletta, 'The Body of the City: Angela Carter's *The Passion of New Eve*', *Science Fiction Studies*, 21:3 (1994), 365–79.

Warner, Marina, *From the Beast to the Blonde: On Fairy Tales and their Tellers* (London: Chatto & Windus, 1994).

Williams, Linda Ruth, *Critical Desire: Psychoanalysis and the Literary Subject* (London: Edward Arnold, 1995).

Wisker, Gina, 'Winged Women and Werewolves: How do we read Angela Carter?' *Ideas and Production*, 4 (1985), 89.

Wisker, Gina, 'Weaving Our Own Web: Demythologising/Remythologising and Magic in the Work of Contemporary Women Writers', in Gina Wisker, ed., *It's My Party: Reading Twentieth Century Women's Writing* (London: Pluto Press, 1994), 104–28.

Zipes, Jack, *The Great Refusal: Studies of the Romantic Hero in German and American Literature* (Bad Homburg: Athenaum Verlag Gmbtl, 1970).

## Reviews

Ackroyd, Peter, 'Passion Fruit', *Spectator*, 238/7760, 26 Mar. 1977, 23–4.

Bailey, Paul, 'Vanishing Island', *Observer*, 24 Nov. 1985, 28.

Banks, Carolyn, 'Angela Carter's Flights of Fancy,' *Washington Post*, 3 Feb. 1985, 1–13.

Bannon, Barbara A., 'The Bloody Chamber', *Publisher's Weekly*, 10 Dec. 1979, 55.

Bayley, John, 'Fighting for the Crown', *New York Review of Books*, 39/8, 23 Apr. 1992, 9–11.

Beesley, Paddy, 'Be Bad', *New Statesman*, 93/2401, 25 Mar. 1977, 407.

Boston, Richard, 'Logic in a Schizophrenic's World', *New York Times Book Review*, 2 Mar. 1969, 42.

Bowen, John, 'Grotesques', *New York Times Book Review*, 19 Feb. 1967.

Brockway, James, 'Gothic Pyrotechnics', *Books and Bookmen*, 20/5, Feb. 1975, 55–6.

Coleman, John, 'From Behind the Wall', *Observer*, 16 May 1971, 33.

Craig, Patricia, 'Gory', *New Statesman*, 97/2514, 25 May 1979, 762.

Cunningham, Valentine, 'High-Wire Fantasy', *Observer*, 30 Sept. 1984, 20.

—— 'Country Coloureds', *Listener*, 87/2252, 25 May 1972, 693.

Enright, D. J., 'Writers at Play', *New York Review of Books*, 34/3, 26 Feb. 1987, 15–16.

Fremont-Smith, Eliot, 'Shock Disarmed', *New York Times*, 3 Feb. 1967, 29.

Friedman, Alan, 'Pleasure and Pain', *New York Times Book Review*, 17 Feb. 1980, 14–15.

Glendinning, Victoria, 'Real Cities', *New Statesman*, 88/2265, 16 Aug. 1974, 229.

Greenwood, Gillian, 'Flying Circus', *Literary Review*, 43, Oct. 1984, 43.

Hamilton, Ian, 'Comfortably Surreal', *Listener*, 78/1998, 13 July 1967, 57.

Hay, George, 'Marionettes with Metaphysics', *Foundation*, 3 Mar. 1973, 69–71.

Hemmings, John, 'Alice in Dropoutland', *Listener*, 80/2053, 1 Aug. 1968, 152.

Hjortsberg, William, *New York Times Book Review*, 8 Sept. 1974.

Hood, Stuart, 'Silly Woman', *Listener*, 82/2120, 13 Nov. 1969, 674.

*Independent on Sunday*, 'Expletives Deleted', 22 Mar. 1992, 26–7.

Ingoldby, Grace, 'Putting on the Style', *New Statesman*, 110/2847, 18 Oct. 1985, 28–9.

Kennedy, Susan, 'Man and Beast', *Times Literary Supplement*, 4011, 8 Feb. 1980, 146.

Krauss, Jennifer, 'History and Histrionics', *New Republic*, 195/25, 22 Dec. 1986, 38–41.

Lee, Hermione, 'Angela Carter's Profane Pleasures', *Times Literary Supplement*, 4655, 19 June 1992, 5–6.

Mars-Jones, Adam, 'From Wonders to Prodigies', *Times Literary Supplement*, 4252, 28 Sept. 1984, 1083.

Mellors, John, 'Kites and Aeroplanes', *Listener*, 92, 26 Sept. 1974, 416.

*New Yorker*, 'The Magic Toyshop', 44/1, 24 Feb. 1968, 133–4.

Phillipson, John S., 'Heroes and Villains', *Best Sellers*, 30/11, 1 Sept. 1970, 211–2.

Potoker, Edward M., 'A Gallery of Grotesques,' *Saturday Review*, 50/7, 18 Feb. 1967, 36.

Rushdie, Salman, 'Brixton Riot Beneath the Greasepaint's Roar', *Independent on Sunday*, 16 June 1991.

Sage, Lorna, 'Glass Menagerie,' *Observer*, 27 Mar. 1977, 29.

—— 'Breaking the Spell of the Past', *Times Literary Supplement*, 4307, 18 Oct. 1985, 1169.

Snitow, Ann, 'The Post-Lapsarian Eve', *Nation*, 243/10, 4 Oct. 1986, 315–7.

—— 'A Footman at the Door', *Nation*, 254/15, 2 Apr. 1992, 526–9.

*Times Literary Supplement*, 'Black Innocence', 3466, 1 Aug. 1968, 817.

*Times Literary Supplement*, 'Facing the Past', 3534, 20 Nov. 1969, 1329.

*Times Literary Supplement*, 'Private Lives', 3661, 18 June 1971, 693.

*Times Literary Supplement*, 'Only Reflect', 3781, 23 Aug. 1974, 897.

Van Vactor, Anita, 'Unceasingly Thankful', *Listener*, 85/2199, 20 May 1971, 656.

Wakeman, John, 'Dark Fantasy', *New York Times Book Review*, 25 Feb. 1968, 38.

Waugh, Auberon, 'The Surreal Thing', *Spectator*, 228/7508, 20 May 1972, 772–3.

Wood, Michael, 'Stories of Black and White', *London Review of Books*, 6/18, 4 Oct. 1984, 16–17.

## Special Issues Devoted to Angela Carter
The Review of Contemporary Fiction, 14:3 (fall 1994).

Marvels and Tales: *Journal of Fairy-Tale Studies*, 12:1 (1998).

## OTHER RELEVANT WORKS
Bakhtin, Mikhail, *Rabelais and His World* (1965); trans. Helene Iswolsky (Bloomington: Indiana University Press, 1984).

—— *Problems of Dostoyevsky's Poetics* (1929); trans. Caryl Emerson (Manchester: Manchester University Press, 1984).

Barthes, Roland, *Image-Music-Text*, trans. Stephen Heath (Fontana/ Collins, 1977).

—— *Empire of Signs* (1970); trans. Richard Howard (London: Jonathan Cape, 1983).

—— *The Pleasure of the Text* (1973); trans. R. Miller (New York: Hill and Wang, 1975).

Brooke-Rose, Christine, *Stories, Theories and Things*, (Cambridge: Cambridge University Press, 1991).

Cixous, Hélène, 'The Character of "character"', *New Literary History*, 5 (1974), 383–402.

—— 'Castration or Decapitation?' (1976); trans. A. Kuhn, *Signs*, 7 (1981), 41–55.

Coward, Rosalind, *Our Treacherous Hearts: Why Women Let Men Get Their Way* (London: Faber and Faber), 1992.

Eco, Umberto, with Rorty, Richard, Culler, Jonathan, and Brooke-Rose, Christine, *Interpretation and Over-Interpretation*, ed. S. Collini (Cambridge: Cambridge University Press, 1992).

Foucault, Michel, *Madness and Civilization: A History of Insanity in the Age of Reason* (1961); trans. Richard Howard (London: Routledge, 1990).
—— *Discipline and Punish* (1973); trans. Alan Sheridan (Harmondsworth: Penguin, 1979).
—— *The History of Sexuality*, i, (1976); trans. Robert Hurley (Harmondsworth: Penguin, 1981).
Gould, Stephen Jay, *Wonderful Life: The Burgess Shale and the Nature of History* (1989; Hutchinson-Radius, 1990).
Hutcheon, Linda, *The Politics of Postmodernism* (London: Routledge, 1989).
Lévi-Strauss, Claude, *Tristes Tropiques* (1955; London: Jonathan Cape, 1973).
—— *The Raw and the Cooked* (1964); trans. John Weightman (London: Jonathan Cape, 1970).
Marcuse, Herbert, *Eros and Civilization* (1955; Boston: Beacon Press, 1966).
—— *One-Dimensional Man* (1964: London: Routledge, 1991).
Sontag, Susan, *A Susan Sontag Reader* (New York: Vintage Books, 1983).
Steiner, George, *Real Presences* (London: Faber and Faber, 1989).
Warner, Marina, *Monuments and Maidens* (1985: London: Picador, 1987).
Yates, Frances, *Giordano Bruno and the Hermetic Tradition* (1964; Chicago: University of Chicago Press, 1991).
—— *The Rosicrucian Enlightenment* (1972; London Ark Paperbacks; 1986).
Zipes, Jack, *Breaking the Magic Spell: Radical Theories of Folk and Fairy Tales* (London: Heinemann, 1979).
—— (ed.) *The Trials and Tribulations of Little Red Riding Hood* (New York and London: Routledge, 1993).

# Index

# Recent and
# Forthcoming Titles
# in the
# New Series of

# WRITERS AND
# THEIR WORK

*"...this series promises to outshine its own
previously high reputation."*
**Times Higher Education Supplement**

*"...will build into a fine multi-volume critical
encyclopaedia of English literature."*
**Library Review & Reference Review**

*"...Excellent, informative, readable, and recommended."*
**NATE News**

*"written by outstanding contemporary critics,
whose expertise is flavoured by unashamed enthusiasm for
their subjects and the series' diverse aspirations."*
**Times Educational Supplement**

*"A useful and timely addition to the ranks of the lit crit and
reviews genre. Written in an accessible and authoritative style."*
**Library Association Record**

# WRITERS AND THEIR WORK

## RECENT & FORTHCOMING TITLES

# RECENT & FORTHCOMING TITLES

| Title | Author |
|---|---|
| English Translators of Homer | *Simeon Underwood* |
| J. G. Farrell | *John McLeod* |
| Henry Fielding | *Jenny Uglow* |
| Veronica Forrest-Thomson – | |
| Language Poetry | *Alison Mark* |
| E. M. Forster | *Nicholas Royle* |
| John Fowles | *William Stephenson* |
| Brian Friel | *Geraldine Higgins* |
| Athol Fugard | *Dennis Walder* |
| Elizabeth Gaskell | *Kate Flint* |
| The *Gawain*-Poet | *John Burrow* |
| The Georgian Poets | *Rennie Parker* |
| William Golding 2/e | *Kevin McCarron* |
| Graham Greene | *Peter Mudford* |
| Neil M. Gunn | *J. B. Pick* |
| Ivor Gurney | *John Lucas* |
| *Hamlet* 2/e | *Ann Thompson & Neil Taylor* |
| Thomas Hardy 2/e | *Peter Widdowson* |
| Tony Harrison | *Joe Kelleher* |
| William Hazlitt | *J. B. Priestley; R. L. Brett* |
| | *(intro. by Michael Foot)* |
| Seamus Heaney 2/e | *Andrew Murphy* |
| *Henry IV* | *Laurence Lerner* |
| George Herbert | *T.S. Eliot (intro. by Peter Porter)* |
| Geoffrey Hill | *Andrew Roberts* |
| Gerard Manley Hopkins | *Daniel Brown* |
| Ted Hughes | *Susan Bassnett* |
| Henrik Ibsen 2/e | *Sally Ledger* |
| Kazuo Ishiguro 2/e | *Cynthia Wong* |
| Henry James – The Later Writing | *Barbara Hardy* |
| James Joyce 2/e | *Steven Connor* |
| *Julius Caesar* | *Mary Hamer* |
| Franz Kafka | *Michael Wood* |
| John Keats | *Kelvin Everest* |
| James Kelman | *Gustav Klaus* |
| Rudyard Kipling | *Jan Montefiore* |
| Hanif Kureishi | *Ruvani Ranasinha* |
| Samuel Johnson | *Liz Bellamy* |
| William Langland: *Piers Plowman* | *Claire Marshall* |
| *King Lear* | *Terence Hawkes* |
| Philip Larkin 2/e | *Laurence Lerner* |
| D. H. Lawrence | *Linda Ruth Williams* |
| Doris Lessing | *Elizabeth Maslen* |
| C. S. Lewis | *William Gray* |
| Wyndham Lewis and Modernism | *Andrzej Gasiorak* |
| David Lodge | *Bernard Bergonzi* |
| *Macbeth* | *Kate McLuskie* |
| Louis MacNeice | *Richard Brown* |
| Katherine Mansfield | *Andrew Bennett* |
| Christopher Marlowe | *Thomas Healy* |
| Andrew Marvell | *Annabel Patterson* |
| Ian McEwan 2/e | *Kiernan Ryan* |
| *Measure for Measure* | *Kate Chedgzoy* |
| *The Merchant of Venice* | *Warren Chernaik* |

# RECENT & FORTHCOMING TITLES

| Title | Author |
|---|---|
| Middleton and His Collaborators | *Hutchings & Bromham* |
| *A Midsummer Night's Dream* | *Helen Hackett* |
| John Milton | *Nigel Smith* |
| Alice Munro | *Ailsa Cox* |
| Vladimir Nabokov | *Neil Cornwell* |
| V. S. Naipaul | *Suman Gupta* |
| New Woman Writers | *Marion Shaw/Lyssa Randolph* |
| Grace Nichols | *Sarah Lawson-Welsh* |
| Edna O'Brien | *Amanda Greenwood* |
| Flann O'Brien | *Joe Brooker* |
| Ben Okri | *Robert Fraser* |
| George Orwell | *Douglas Kerr* |
| *Othello* | *Emma Smith* |
| Walter Pater | *Laurel Brake* |
| Brian Patten | *Linda Cookson* |
| Caryl Phillips | *Helen Thomas* |
| Harold Pinter | *Mark Batty* |
| Sylvia Plath 2/e | *Elisabeth Bronfen* |
| Pope Amongst the Satirists | *Brean Hammond* |
| Revenge Tragedies of the Renaissance | *Janet Clare* |
| Jean Rhys 2/e | *Helen Carr* |
| *Richard II* | *Margaret Healy* |
| *Richard III* | *Edward Burns* |
| Dorothy Richardson | *Carol Watts* |
| John Wilmot, Earl of Rochester | *Germaine Greer* |
| *Romeo and Juliet* | *Sasha Roberts* |
| Christina Rossetti | *Kathryn Burlinson* |
| Salman Rushdie 2/e | *Damian Grant* |
| Paul Scott | *Jacqueline Banerjee* |
| The Sensation Novel | *Lyn Pykett* |
| P. B. Shelley | *Paul Hamilton* |
| Sir Walter Scott | *Harriet Harvey Wood* |
| Iain Sinclair | *Robert Sheppard* |
| Christopher Smart | *Neil Curry* |
| Wole Soyinka | *Mpalive Msiska* |
| Muriel Spark | *Brian Cheyette* |
| Edmund Spenser | *Colin Burrow* |
| Gertrude Stein | *Nicola Shaughnessy* |
| Laurence Sterne | *Manfred Pfister* |
| Bram Stoker | *Andrew Maunder* |
| Graham Swift | *Peter Widdowson* |
| Jonathan Swift | *Ian Higgins* |
| Swinburne | *Catherine Maxwell* |
| Elizabeth Taylor | *N. R. Reeve* |
| Alfred Tennyson | *Seamus Perry* |
| W. M. Thackeray | *Richard Salmon* |
| D. M. Thomas | *Bran Nicol* |
| Three Lyric Poets | *William Rowe* |
| J. R. R. Tolkien | *Charles Moseley* |
| Leo Tolstoy | *John Bayley* |
| Charles Tomlinson | *Tim Clark* |
| Anthony Trollope | *Andrew Sanders* |
| Victorian Quest Romance | *Robert Fraser* |
| Marina Warner | *Laurence Coupe* |